*footnote;

A Literary Journal of History

· Various Authors ·

Alternating Current
Palo Alto, California

Footnote No. 1
Various Authors
©2015 Alternating Current

Front cover artwork: "Mr. Sunshine." Back cover artwork: "Business as Usual." Artwork by Terry Fan of Terry Fan Illustration, society6.com/igo2cairo. Property of and ©2015 Terry Fan Illustration and used with permission; all rights reserved.

The Featured Writer photographs are acknowledged as follows: A. Jay Adler by Julia Dean, and Jesseca Cornelson by John Morrow. Both photographs are ©2015 their respective creators and used with permission; all rights reserved. All other photographs in public domain.

Design and Editor: Leah Angstman
leahangstman.com

Technical Graphics Editor: Michael Litos

Alternating Current
Palo Alto, California

For the most current contact and ordering information, visit:
alternatingcurrentarts.com

ISBN-10: 0692479228
ISBN-13: 978-0692479223
First Edition: August 2015

*If you don't know where you've come from,
you don't know where you are.*

—James Burke

the Editor

History. Inside that word is wrapped nearly everything I love in life. As an author of historical fiction and historical metered verse, I cannot help but dive into my research with a whole heart and feel fulfilled at the findings in a way that changes me every time, for the better even when it seems for the worse. I am the type who does not wish to change history, to hide from it, to fight it or to whitewash it or to revere it or to misquote it or to misinterpret it. I appreciate and respect her as she stands, ugly and gorgeous. Seeing events, places, people, and ideas in their elements, in their atmospheres and environments, to be able to freeze them in time and say, "This is how it was. This is what we know," is a privilege I take very seriously, and that I pass on to others as responsibly as human nature will allow. As a writer who actively submits to publications, I have noticed an absence of history in the independent literary scene. Editors seem to chronicle the here and now, coddle the experimental over the fact, the abstract and dystopian over personal connections to the past. My writing is often slow to find a home because historical pieces are deemed inaccessible to people who have not cracked open that particular history text, often deemed too educational or scholarly by journals that expect entertainment and bleeding hearts over concrete connections to a sordid past that can generally be a downer, or worse ... controversial, heavy, or very unpleasant altogether. But what does an author do when that writing isn't pretentiously academic or something that would grace the glossy pages of *American History* or *Smithsonian*, yet isn't considered accessible enough for editors looking for modern literary pieces? Welcome to *Footnote*, a space built for those personal and non-scholarly viewpoints of historical people, places, events, or ideas that struggle to find a space elsewhere, out of context. This is a home for history enthusiasts, writers, and readers. And judging by the amount of submissions received and authors who voiced the same sentiments, I have learned that I am not alone in the need for this space, this home. Please enjoy your romp through the parts of our pasts that haunt, amaze, and intrigue us, giving voice to the good and bad, ugly and lovely, objective and emotional—but rarely indifferent. There are moments of discomfort, but we are firm believers that history is not meant merely to entertain, but to educate. Only through knowledge and discussion can we repeat the good, while never forgetting the ugly.

Table of

CONTENTS

MATTER

My Father Tells Us about Leaving Vilnius

LYN LIFSHIN

On the night we left Vilnius, I had to bring goats
next door in the moon. Since I was not the youngest, I
couldn't wait pressed under a shawl of coarse cotton
close to Mama's breast as she whispered, "Hurry," in Yiddish.
Her ankles were swollen from ten babies. Though she was
only thirty, her waist was thick, her lank hair hung in strings

under the babushka she swore she would burn in New York
City. She dreamed others pointed and snickered near the
tenement, that a neighbor borrowed the only bowl she
brought that was her mother's and broke it. That night, every
move had to be secret. In rooms there was no heat in, no one
put on muddy shoes or talked. It was forbidden to leave,

a law we broke like the skin of ice on pails of milk. Years from
then, a daughter would write that I didn't have a word for
America yet, that night of a new moon. Mother pressed my
brother to her, warned everyone even the babies must not make
a sound. Frozen branches creaked. I shivered at men with
guns near straw roofs on fire. It took our old samovar every

coin to bribe someone to take us to the train. "Pretend to be
sleeping," father whispered as the conductor moved near. Mother
stuffed cotton in the baby's mouth. She held the mortar and
pestle wrapped in my quilt of feathers closer, told me I would
sleep in this soft blue in the years ahead. But that
night, I was knocked sideways into ribs of the
boat, so seasick I couldn't swallow the
orange someone threw from an upstairs
bunk, though it was bright as sun and
smelled of a new country I could only
imagine, though never how my mother
would become a stranger to herself
there, forget why we risked dogs
and guns to come.

The Romanov Family Portrait

CHRISTINA ELAINE COLLINS

At midnight,
gunfire breathes on the prison house. Yurovsky,
leader of the executioners, focuses on the brow
of the family doctor. He explains:
In view of the unrest in the town,
it has become necessary
to move the Romanov family

> *downstairs.*

A barred window
ornaments a bare room, eleven feet by thirteen. Yurovsky
leads them in for a painless
photograph: first Nicholas, carrying his frail
son; then Alexandra and the girls, following
in worthless dresses, hoping they might disappear
into a ballroom. Sugarcoated
bullets spurt from the leader's lips: *Please, you stand*
here, and you here … That's it,

> *in a row.*

The family waits
with shoulders back, grander still
in degradation. A family photograph
might yet lift Nicky's drooping
mustache—a reason to smile. He stands close to
the ones he loves
more than the country

> he lost.

Time
to summon the photographer. At Yurovsky's
orders he enters, without a camera. He is
eleven men armed with revolvers. Yurovsky
looms before the last czar, a scrap of paper
in his palm, his voice calm.

In view of the fact
that your relatives

Smile for the family portrait.

are continuing their attack
on Soviet Russia,

This moment will live, but

the Ural Executive Committee
has decided

you will not.

The Romanovs

13

Lara to Yurii Andreievich*

DIANA ANDRASI

In war, the roulette is the only queen.
Let it spin
with grin
and exhaustion.

The words are yours.
Mine is just the death.
With deep Northern frost, I bend my eyes
to collect the life drops.
In blue and white cap, the winter goes around to show off
its new vintage collection.
On top of the hill, dressed up like a cheap whore,
the revolution.
At the mansion's door, a Cossack casket
with lipstick embroidery
winks majestically to the shy comrade ...

I've lost you in the forest,
  I've found you in the blood field with twisted veins
and crooked skin.
If, by any chance, you see that tall lady with hissing name—
History, tell her the truth.
She must know it. For the sake of the emptiness.
Winter and revolution, they catch the same disease: cold at heart.

~

You put the gods in order
and the humans back in their bodies;
With years, you find yourself alone,
and you blame the fate for it.
In fact, it isn't the fate, but the blue of the sky
or the flow in the blood
or just the insignificance of the daily breath
or the voice of a lost bee.

---

* *Known as "Doctor Zhivago"*

In your pockets, the big revolution shaped like small clinking change:
silvery unvalued coins
with letters and flags,
to be grasped by some oily, stinky fingers.
The activists are singing in falsetto.
In the name of the freedom and the people.
Meanwhile, in my bed, short intermissions of your sick, radical bones.

Making love was never so revolutionary.

~

In the North, for some, blindness is red. For others, is white.
In the turmoil, colors have failed you.
Happiness has fooled you.
Yet, the orders were clear,
sentences short,
decrees inconsistent,
names misspelled,
while winter was standing tall in the kitchen door.
Let's borrow a pair of scissors
to trim, like mad tailors, the sleeves and cleavage of Sankt-Petersburg.
The ruins left around human screams and bleedings
grow like moss in the shadows.
Silence creeps inside your poems
to soften the rhythm of sorrow.

The last time, you were standing on the veranda,
your coat over one shoulder,
clutching desperately the frosted rail.
Setting sun over the other shoulder.
Hunger howling in the distance.
Thumping heart with shaking knees.
Standing-still snow.
Missing Moscow.
Pain swallowing into the cold air.
Challenging God.
Making sure that "gone" is gone.
Sense sharpening to wave farewell ...

The revolution is not the make of fanatical men,
but the swollen root of illusion.
There isn't anything more schizophrenic than the revolution.

15

~

After the Red politics died silently
and the people kept forgetting the screams and the bleedings,
after Lenin burnt his crown and melted his brains
and new men with new red blood in the lungs
stood up for the new brave world,
you wrapped yourself in words
to embalm the spring of the verse.

Poetry was never again so Russian.

Pogrom

Kneeling, in damp clay,
my fingers brush
tender shoots of crocus.

For an eternity, I fondle
those frail, green fronds,
so full of spring, of promise.

I water them with my tears.

Finally, someone is shouting.
The sky, a pit,
yawns, cloudless, overhead.

I open my senses to the sky.
—What is this place?—
I turn, falling endlessly forward.

LUTHER JETT

The Dictionary

O

obedient   obey   obituary
object   objectify   obligatory
obliterate   oblivion

O forms in the mouth,
in the throat, above the tongue:

an outward movement of air,
a hollow, round sound.

Open the page at letter O.
See what you find.

Oancea, Gheorghe. Peasant. Sentenced to 15 years.

Oancea, Ion. Peasant. Arrested with his son Stefan, teacher. Tortured by Securitate. Sentenced to 10 years and his son to 5 years. Wife Agmira and the other 2 children deported for 6 years to forced labor camps (stone quarries).

Oancea, Soare. From Bessarabia. Arrested by NKVD and deported to Siberia in 1946.
No further information avail.

Oancea, Traian I. Student at the Polytechnic Institute. Sentenced to 8 years for conspiracy against social order.

Oancea, Vasile. Tortured by Securitate. Sentenced to 5 years. Wife Floarea and 2 children deported.

Oancea, Zosima. Priest. Married, father of 4 minors. Arrested because he helped the families of political prisoners. Sentenced to 9 years.

Name:
a succession of sounds
to which a face is attached.

The name might as well be spelled
by vowels, clangs of shackles,
consonants, thuds
of fists against skin,
bangs of prison doors, rattle
of cattle trains.

observe   obsessed   obsolete
obstacle   obstinate   occupied   occur
ocean   oculus   ocular

Ocular. Eye. Eyewitness.

> Obancea, Gheorghe. Arrested for giving food to partisans.
> Tortured by Securitate. Sentenced to 15 years forced labor.
>
> Obarseanu, Florea I. Peasant. Arrested on October 21, 1959,
> for activities against land nationalization. Tortured by
> Securitate. Sentenced to 5 years.
>
> Oberding, Dominic. Arrested by NKVD and sent to forced
> labor camps in Siberia.
>
> Oberkirch, Barbara. Born in 1934. Arrested by NKVD and
> sent to forced labor camps in Siberia, where she died.
>
> Oberkirch, Magdalena. Deported since 1951.
>
> Obician, Arcadia, Dragutin, Dusan, Mara. Peasants.
> Deported on June 18, 1951.

odious   offend   offensive
official   often   old   omen
ominous   omission   only   one

Only one. The one.
Every one is *the* one.
The only one.

They once had bodies,
flesh, voice, life.

19

Now all that remains
are lists of names,
bones in a cemetery online.

> Olaru, Aurelia. Born on August 19, 1941. Arrested on May 5,
> 1952, 11 years old. Deported.
>
> Olaru, Constantin. Born in 1929. From Bessarabia. Deported
> to Siberia (Kurgan) with his wife Alexandra on July 6, 1949.
>
> Olaru, Constantin I. Worker. Arrested with his father Ion and
> brother Stefan in 1949. His cooperation with the investigators
> resulted in multiple arrests.
>
> Olaru, Petre. Arrested because of statements made by his son.
> Interrogated by Securitate, where he was beaten by his own
> son.

ongoing   onslaught   on purpose
open   operate   operative
oppose   opposition   oppressive

Faces blurred,
eaten by time.

O forms in the mouth
that blows binary dust across
the computer screen,
byte by byte.

Names, names,
enough to populate a small country
of pain.

But do you hear them scream?

> Oprescu, Gheorghe I. Born on October 28, 1934. Sentenced to
> 5 years for conspiracy against social order, then deported.
>
> Oprescu, Grigore S. Sentenced to 2 years forced labor.
>
> Oprescu, Puiu. Economist. Sentenced to 7 years.
>
> Oprescu, Toma. Priest. Sentenced to 8 years.

Opret, Iacob. Peasant. Arrested in December 1956. Tortured during interrogation. Sentenced to 7 years forced labor.

Opris, Constantin. Lawyer. Sentenced to 5 years in 1950. Arrested again in 1958 and sentenced to 24 years forced labor.

opprobrium   opprobrious   ordain   ordeal
order   orderly   orphan   ostracize   our

Our. Our Father,
Who art in heaven,
Holy is Thy Name.

My father
and his father and brothers.

Our. Our fathers.
Our grandfathers, uncles, brothers.
Their names.

> Opris, Ilie. Greek-Catholic priest. Killed during interrogation.
>
> Opris, Nicolae. Arrested because he helped several people cross the border to Yugoslavia. Sentenced to 12 years.
>
> Oprisan, Constantin Costache. Sentenced to forced labor for life.
>
> Oprita, Ileana. Born on January 1, 1951. Arrested in 1958 (7 years old) and deported.
>
> Oprita, Octavian. College student and partisan. Killed by Securitate in Apuseni Mountains.
>
> Oproiu, Ion. Arrested with his father (priest, 74 years old) for refusing nationalization. Sentenced to 20 years forced labor.

O forms in my mouth
and in my bones.

O forms in the way my hair follows
the oval of my face,
my father's forehead,
my grandfather's nose.

My blood carries Os.

Search: trialofcommunism.com/
testimonials/
arrested, tortured, imprisoned, killed/
dictionary/N-O/

Scroll down to Orasel,
my maiden name.
It means *small town.*

> Orasel, Eliodor V. Born in 1939. Sentenced to 8 years for
> conspiracy against social order.

> Orasel, Lucian V. Born in 1937. Sentenced in 1956 to 10
> years.

> Orasel, Petre Gh. Sentenced to 6 years for conspiracy against
> social order.

> Orasel, Vasile. Father of Eliodor and Lucian. Sentenced to 25
> years for refusing nationalization of the land.

oust   out   outcast   outlaw   outwear
over   overflow   overkill   overwhelm

O, the sound of wind
winding through the hollow of bones.

Chain links, chained Os.
Eyes. The round eyes,
the fixated pupils of death.

> Orban, Andrei. Butcher. Killed during detention, in 1951.

> Orban, Carol. Accountant. Sentenced to death and executed
> on September 1, 1958.

> Orban, Cornel. Sentenced to death in 1956. Executed on
> September 1, 1958.

> Orban, Stefan. Sentenced to death in 1956. Executed on
> September 1, 1958.

> Ordeanu, Danila. Worker. Arrested in 1951. Killed in the
> Cernavoda camp, on February 9, 1953.

Orendi, Ioan I. Clerk. Arrested in 1950. Killed during detention in 1952.

Who stole their years,
their lives? Who?

Letters ignite into funeral fires.

The dead are baking ovals of bread.

My grandmother places
torn pieces of meat
into the gaping O
of the pot on the stove.

Oh, the stories untold.

Orescu, Gheorghe V. From Bessarabia. Deported in camps from Irkutsk, Siberia, with wife Maia and children Fiodor, Varvara, and Ecaterina.

Orezeanu, I. County clerk. Arrested by NKVD and deported to forced labor camps in Pecioara, Komi region, Siberia.

Organ, Alexandra E. From Bessarabia. Peasant. Deported to camps from Cita region with children Vasilisa and Victor.

Organ, Ivan I. From Bessarabia. Peasant. Deported to camps from Cita region with wife Feodosia and children Alexandru and Alexei.

Organ, Vasile. From Bessarabia. Peasant. Deported to camps from Kurgan region with wife Eudochia and son Andrei.

overrun   overswarm   overthrow
overturn   own   own up

My own drops,
small drops
in an ocean of Os.

I owe them words,
own,   own up.

Own up to the Os.

"Along with Jovan Dučić and Milan Rakić, Vojislav Ilić (1860-1894) is one of the three best lyricists of rhymed poetry in Serbian. Since he is the oldest of the three, and since he died much younger than the other two, he is seen as a figure that influenced both Dučić and Rakić, as he did scores of other poets both in his time and in the wake of his passage over to the Elysium (which is one of many classicist references he used; yet, he broke with Romanticism resolutely, espousing formalist æstheticism, but never—as Dučić will be accused half a century later—at the expense of emotion in his poetry).

Vojislav Ilić was a major poetic influence on me when growing up. For years, I considered him the peak of what one could do with literary Serbian language. Indeed, he prepared me for British Pre-Raphaelite and French fin-de-siècle poetry, and his openness about the world—which was rather harsh to him during his relatively short life—sowed a seed of globe-trotting in my soul at an impressionable pre-teen age, which resulted in my living for a year or longer in eight countries on three continents in the last 20 years."

—*Miodrag Kojadinović*

Hearing, oh Hearing, the Wailing of the World*

(To Vojislav)

Your refined æstheticism made the country
whose citizenship I held, but whose political
system I abhorred, worthy of love. Your respect
and empathy for the old peasant granny, feeding
the chickens, presaged your—and my—more
modern fellow poet Różewicz's woman pulling
the goat on a string, "more needed, worth more
than the seven wonders of the world."

In your "On the Ionian Sea Coast," more than
in the black and white photo of a group of people
standing in front of monuments—faculty
of the school at which Mom taught on a coach tour
of Greece—and more than in Melina Mercouri
never doing *it* on a Sunday, did I find rationale
and enticement to invoke Brother Sun at Delphi,
to dream at Sounion, to roam the alleyways of Piraeus.

Your itinerant bohemianism matched my search
for positions teaching abroad, my uprootedness
and work for embassies, albeit foreign, while
you served your king's consulates abroad.

I remember: it was your Tibulus, watching,
mesmerized, the cold beauty of the marble Venus
in the times of—of all emperors—Elagabalus,
that had set me on the road to my élitist difference.

---

* *"Hear, oh hear, the wind as it wails*
through the fields of the land, rolling tufts
of heavy fog down into the humid valley …"
is the first couplet of the poem, "Autumn," by Vojislav Ilić,
one of his best-known works.

MIODRAG KOJADINOVIĆ

Millions of verses of poets as variegated as Lorca,
Pessoa, Li Bai, Rilke, Swinburne, and Bashō later,
in my mind's eye I still go to the safety
of the somber and empty, but well-known,
faculty room at Mom's school, where Father
would drive us on a windy early morning,
and I would wait for my own class to start
in the building half a block away, half an hour later
reading your poems, admiring your perfectly
chiseled verse, while not always understanding
every reference to Ancient Greece, Rome,
Pan-Slavonic deities, historic and social issues
of your time, that made you a diplomat and a political
prisoner, time bygone for three quarters of a
century before I was born, and I would dream
of the worlds to discover, thanks to you, Vojislav.

Vojislav Ilić

Tibulus / Тибуло

Under the darkness of a quiet night, young Tibulus,
a *quiritus*, stood silent before a statue of Venus in awe
and beheld the strange appearance. While the eternal city
rested in a deserved sleep, his dreamy gaze away to draw
the youth could not from a sight
so strange—the marvelous workmanship possessed him
with a strange might.
Thus it dawned, yet he stood awake, and after a time
darkness once again came down as if a woman
letting her hair loose. And he dreamed alone until he was
startled with a murmur, rebuking him through the Roman
bustling city. He heard the tone:
Oh, wretched Tibulus, our boy! May gods have mercy
on him, the lover of a cold stone!

~

Пред хладни Венусов кип, под сенком питоме ноћи,
Тибуло, квирит млад, зачуђен застаде немо,
И чудни гледаше лик. На крилу одмора свога
Ромула вечни град спокојно, тихо је дремô,
А квирит стоји млад,
И с чудне статуе те сањиве не своди очи,
И гледа бајни рад. —
И зора сину већ, а он је стојао будан,
И снова тавна ноћ распусти чаробне власи,
А он је сневао сан — и прекор из сна га трже,
Кроз бурни, цели град, што тајни збораху гласи,
И он је чуо сам:
Несрећни Тибуло наш, богови нека га штите!
Он љуби хладни кам.

VOJISLAV ILIĆ

TRANSLATED BY
MIODRAG KOJADINOVIĆ

Исповест

(Excerpt)

VOJISLAV ILIĆ / ВОЈИСЛАВ ИЛИЋ

На трошном чуну, без крме и наде,
У мени вера губи се и мре;
Ја више ништа не верујем, ништа
Ил' боље рећи: ја верујем све.

На мору бурном људскога живота
Прерано ја сам упознао свет:
За мене живот ништавна је сенка,
За мене живот отрован је цвет.

Трпи и живи … Пријатељу драги,
О много чему мислио сам ја —
О благо оном, ко не мисли ништа,
Тај мање тужи, мање јада зна

~

Бурне су страсти извор многих зала,
Несрећи људској почетак је страст;
Море живота оне страсно муте,
Над људском душом њихова је власт.

~

Све, што год живи-свом се паду клони
Променом време означава ход;
Оно нам даје веру и обара,
Слаби и снажи цео људски род.

Confession

(Excerpt)

The boat is frail; it has no stern. Hope is gone
in me, faith is dwindling, faith is dying.
Nay, in nothing do I believe anymore, none,
though one could as easily say: believe in anything.

On the high seas of human life, 't was too early
that I had to learn of what makes the world tick:
now for me life is but a shadow cast, unworthy,
a poisonous flower is life, that makes one sick.

"Suffer and carry on ..." Oh, my beloved friend,
so many dark thoughts have weighed me down.
Lucky is the one who can insouciance withstand,
for he is spared from sadness, sighs, and frown.

~

Tumultuous passions have brought me wretched pain,
for passion lies at the root of human misery,
as it unsettles the seas of our lives in vain,
and has dominion over the man's soul, every.

~

And yet all that is quick will once be dead,
fall is the ultimate measure of temporal flair.
Time doeth give us faith first, then despair,
first strengthens us, then fails us instead.

TRANSLATED BY MIODRAG KOJADINOVIĆ

Turkey / Турска

As if they had lain dead for a long time, before me stretch cities
and quiet, gloomy villages. Around the tops of dark houses and
climbing the ancient stone walls, there winds a heavy trellis; wind
rustles through its leaves high above;
all is covered by it, like ancient cemeteries hidden under the greens.

Behold, too, atop the murky hilltop, there stand centuries-old ruins,
similar to an eerie, gigantic skeleton … Through crumbling former
windows a dreamy wind whispers, and high grasses sprout through
bringing a dreary forgetfulness.

What long years of upheavals have chipped off the surface of
shiny towers and walls now appears as if it had never been
touched by a human hand. In old city's midst, screech-owls nest,
hideous serpents crawl on the floor, and lizards run on the grass.

VOJISLAV ILIĆ

**TRANSLATED BY
MIODRAG KOJADINOVIĆ**

~

Ко изумрли давно, преда мном градови леже
И мирна убога села. Са мрачних домова њини'
И древних, камених платна, вињага густа се вије
Ил' шуми на висини,
И као прастаро гробље лиснатом врежом их крије.

Ено на с야 суром вису урвине вековне стоје
Ко страшан, огроман скелет … Кроз окна њихова пуста
Сањиво шумори ветар и ниче висока трава
Суморног заборава.

Изгледа, као да човек ни руком дотако није,
Што су столећа бурна одбила у мрачном ходу
Са кула и платна градских. Ту гнездо јеина вије,
И змија одвратно мили и гуштер по травном поду.

John Berryman's Rough Rider, Stephen Crane

ALAN CATLIN

("Suddenly Crane, who was incapable of bravado, let himself quietly over the redoubt, lighted a cigarette, stood for a few moments with his arms at his sides, while the bullets hissed past him into the mud, then as quietly climbed back over the redoubt and strolled away. It was impossible, H— said, to question the insouciance of this act: Crane's bearing was that of a somnambulist."
—John Berryman, *Stephen Crane: A Critical Biography*)

What war was it that he was seeing?
Not the Civil one, unless you counted the turmoil
inside, of self against self. He walked like
a dreamer on the field of a Spanish-
American battlefield, but his mind was somewhere
else, among his natural kinsmen, the dead.
Despite the clinical bill of health, the Saranac
doctor's assurance that all would be well,
there could be no doubt that he knew this was
the end, so why not find it here, on a field of
honor, among men who had come to die?
A chosen death at the hands of another might
be the way to a kind of honor, of glory,
he might not otherwise find.
Much easier to walk among the murderers' bullets,
the cannonading shells, explosive shrapnel casings,
completely oblivious and unafraid, than it is
to avoid the inevitability of what waits inside.

A man said to the universe:

A man said to the universe:
"Sir, I exist!"
"However," replied the universe,
"The fact has not created in me
A sense of obligation."

Stephen Crane

Stephen Crane's *Red Badge of Courage*

ALAN CATLIN

Did he, as Keats did, recognize the blood
spots welling from within as the fatal sign?
Or were the words of misplaced reassurance,
from assorted doctors all over the globe, enough
to have faith in? Lying in a cot on the edge
of a Cuban jungle, too weak to move, caught
in the grip of a fevered dream, the sound of
thunder a kind of dread artillery, advancing
from beneath the wavering horizon of sleep,
unleashing fusillade after fusillade, bursting
holes in the clinging mosquito webs around him,
allowing the light, the insects in.
Terror-stricken, reaching for the roll-your-own
tobacco pouch and papers with shaking hands,
he sees himself running, heedless of what lies
ahead, dread, shadow armies in pursuit, waving
drawn sabers that glow, a reflected glint of a
full moonlit night. Striking a match head with
the cracked edges of a thumbnail slows the dream,
the night sweats that subside in the dark.
A sniper sights the red end of the cigarette,
thinking either the smoker is a suicidal madman,
quietly courting death, or a man too brave
to live.

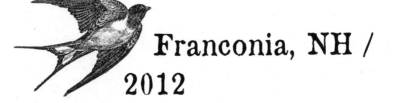

Franconia, NH / 2012

ANTHONY G. HERLES

His mailbox still stands by the gravel road in front of his house.

The flag is up, but he will not be responding.

He is too busy mending walls,

Going out to the pasture,

Bending birches,

Traveling on snowy December nights,

On roads not taken.

Too busy being alive

In thousands of American classrooms.

Robert Frost

The Need of Being Versed in Country Things

ROBERT FROST, 1874-1963

The house had gone to bring again
To the midnight sky a sunset glow.
Now the chimney was all of the house that stood,
Like a pistil after the petals go.

The barn opposed across the way,
That would have joined the house in flame
Had it been the will of the wind, was left
To bear forsaken the place's name.

No more it opened with all one end
For teams that came by the stony road
To drum on the floor with scurrying hoofs
And brush the mow with the summer load.

The birds that came to it through the air
At broken windows flew out and in,
Their murmur more like the sigh we sigh
From too much dwelling on what has been.

Yet for them the lilac renewed its leaf,
And the aged elm, though touched with fire;
And the dry pump flung up an awkward arm;
And the fence post carried a strand of wire.

For them there was really nothing sad.
But though they rejoiced in the nest they kept,
One had to be versed in country things
Not to believe the phoebes wept.

 # Ephemeræ

LUTHER JETT

Only a third of the dinosaur species
that will eventually be discovered
have been found; beyond this,
there are entire species—entire
generæ, that were once plentiful
and fruitful, of which no single
specimen remains. We will never
know these animals existed, nor
of their ways, their secrets, their songs.

And of all the songs of Sappho,
no single complete poem is left—
only fragments. Yet, she fared better
than most. There were great
Tragedians, winners of laurels many
times over, of whose works
not a word has come down to us.
All that labor, all the vanity and
glory—gone, as though
they never were.

One day, you, too, will be forgotten,
who knew my heart as no one
else, before or since, has known it.

Happy Bridegroom / Epithalamium

Happy bridegroom, Hesper brings
All desired and timely things.
All whom morning sends to roam,
Hesper loves to lead them home.
Home return who him behold,
Child to mother, sheep to fold,
Bird to nest from wandering wide:
Happy bridegroom, seek your bride.

SAPPHO, c. 630-570 B.C.E.

TRANSLATED BY
A. E. HOUSMAN

Sappho

Hamlet

DIANA ANDRASI

he failed to kill the killer
and love the lover.
he failed to embrace his mother
and bury his father.
his madness is the dance with ghosts and words.
he lined up the skulls
and pulled out their smiles.

without resentment,
the guards are shouting to the air.

again, the time is out of joints
and father's voice is out of order.
to put up with the history,
one has to sink deeply into insanity
and play the tiptoes of secret languages.

from north-northwest, he's just insane.
from south, he's blue like spring clouds.
in Denmark, ghosts speak of crimes.
in England, they speak of wives.

with patches over broken arms and hearts,
the Dane goes on the scene
to whistle into fight.

Gertrude is the venom.
Ophelia a story,
yet rootless time reigns over them.
the matter is not revenge, nor love or madness,
but history with ghostly voice.

Sonnet LXXXVI (86.)

Was it the proud full sail of his great verse,
Bound for the prize of all too precious you,
That did my ripe thoughts in my brain inhearse,
Making their tomb the womb wherein they grew?
Was it his spirit, by spirits taught to write
Above a mortal pitch, that struck me dead?
No, neither he, nor his compeers by night
Giving him aid, my verse astonished.
He, nor that affable familiar ghost
Which nightly gulls him with intelligence,
As victors of my silence cannot boast;
I was not sick of any fear from thence:
    But when your countenance filled up his line,
    Then lacked I matter; that enfeebled mine.

WILLIAM SHAKESPEARE, 1564-1616

William Shakespeare

Henry Melville, Author, Dead

ALAN CATLIN

Unlike Twain, his river journeys contracted
into ever smaller and more confining state rooms
of the mind, until the last one, more like
a coffin than a room with a bed and a porthole
but just as dark and as inescapable after
lights out, conceived as it was, this series
of interlocking cells, under the shadow of
an hourglass, or was this cell a holding room
for a man about to be brought to the gallows
for a crime he did not willfully commit?
If there is myth involved in this tale of
life, of confidences made and lost, it is of
a man reduced to walking the docks of New York
as a Customs Agent, refusing bribes of convenience,
admitting to no one that the name of the street
that brought him to the harbor was that of a
forebear or that his wife of many years was
heard to remark in his later years,
"He's writing poetry now. Don't tell anyone.
You know how these things get around."
Having failed, on his return to sea,
in the dual quest to recapture the glory of
success and, failing that, self annihilation,
he chose the living kind of oblivion instead,
writing the kinds of books he wanted, convincing
himself that the impenetrable *Pierre: or, The
Ambiguities* was the stuff of Romance, and
the public be damned.
But the public was not damned, and the desultory
books that followed, each more bleak than the
next, achieved nothing.
When he finally died, a broken and bitter man,
his New York obituary read: *Henry Melville,
author, dead*, a last ironic trick of the fateful
Confidence Man, robbing the grave of its
inhabitant even before it is laid to rest.

A Requiem

(For soldiers lost in ocean transports)

When, after storms that woodlands rue,
To valleys comes atoning dawn,
The robins blithe their orchard-sports renew;
And meadowlarks, no more withdrawn
Caroling fly in the languid blue;
The while, from many a hid recess,
Alert to partake the blessedness,
The pouring mites their airy dance pursue.
So, after ocean's ghastly gales,
When laughing light of hoyden morning breaks,
Every finny hider wakes—
From vaults profound swims up with glittering scales;
Through the delightsome sea he sails,
With shoals of shining tiny things
Frolic on every wave that flings
Against the prow its showery spray;
All creatures joying in the morn,
Save them forever from joyance torn,
Whose bark was lost where now the dolphins play;
Save them that by the fabled shore,
Down the pale stream are washed away,
Far to the reef of bones are borne;
And never revisits them the light,
Nor sight of long-sought land and pilot more;
Nor heed they now the lone bird's flight
'Round the lone spar where mid-sea surges pour.

HERMAN MELVILLE, 1819-1891

Rodin's Thinker

DIANA ANDRASI

Long libations from dawn to dusk.
Caught in bronze, the metal's prisoner floats
with feathers attached to memory.
The body of the thinker bends over the space
to protect its heaviness.
Then, it bends over the water to measure its flow.
Then, it bends over the breaths and shrinks
in the last piece of air.
The mystery of struggle stands as effigy.

Inside his casting skin,
like Orpheus' death,
thoughts come in a long line, one by one,
to strike into his solid existence.
With brooding blood, he hits his forehead.
Between the kneecap and the hand cup
the pain's history
in images and songs,
opens up and glows to darkness.

Miraculous nights tell stories to avoid death
and they call for the thinker.
He bends again on the scene,
growls
and goes back into copper.

Human broodiness with metal make-up.

South of North: A Poem Sequence for Nicolas de La Caille

ANGIE JEFFREYS SCHOMP

1.) Physics of the Antigravity

I would like to ignore the gravity of people,
just see you in 2-dimensions, shaded against
page. You do this, record that masses cannot
pull against each other the way hurricanes
spin to shore, then fall to stop.

Mathematically construct a world where
nothing pulls against me except the ground.
I move by connecting a dot-illuminated night,
my fingers run through the vortex lined with
silhouettes.

I sleep there in dreams sometimes, that
asymmetric globe by you, pulling against
the crevices: arms warped by this unfamiliar
force. Mountains behind rain sleep lazily.
They're wrapped around

tools; they circumscribe the hemisphere.
Yet, you create formulas that will never be
repeated: you're an empty house,
uninvented with deliberation. You harness

the light you've stolen from mirror reflections,
and you soldered stars into tools and
fairytale-scientifics, behind the sun risen in front of sky.

2.) Horologium: A Poem in Four Parts

I. The Ancient Greek

Dividing 12 segments of sunlight into equal parts
sun pressed firm against shadows until

hours lie flat like paper rubbings copied carbon
over the bronze sundial in the backyard.

Notches optically alluded onto
fresh turf or patio, hours intangibly fall

and shift into spaces between reflected heat
steamed up from soil or concrete patio, grayed.

I held the sundial blackened green, the shadows blue,
and I was a solitary pole, 6, creating my own notches,

pressed against the rough cement, rocks skinning
my knees as I rotated around myself like the hands of a watch.

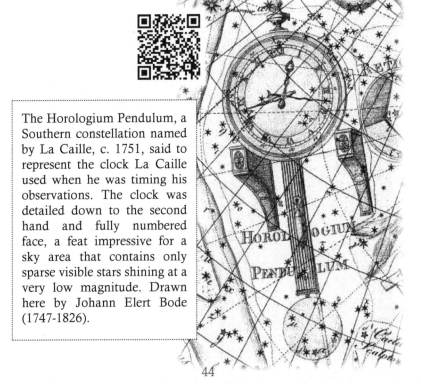

The Horologium Pendulum, a Southern constellation named by La Caille, c. 1751, said to represent the clock La Caille used when he was timing his observations. The clock was detailed down to the second hand and fully numbered face, a feat impressive for a sky area that contains only sparse visible stars shining at a very low magnitude. Drawn here by Johann Elert Bode (1747-1826).

II. Ignore the Night

The night lies unmarked by hours: I wait
in backyard shadows falling onto sundial

between patio floodlights. I invent one mark of an hour
with the light switch by the door, try to mimic the first 12,

count for worn grooves melted away by sunlight
on its face, but now it's only smooth and dry to touch.

The Earth Horologium, the night sky one hour
webbed over cement and patio furniture colors.

A streetlight burns its way through, notching
the ground with thick pools. I stand perpendicular

with the persistence of an insomniac behind daylight
tracing shadows between shadows with my fingers.

Nicolas de La Caille

III. Huygens' Pendulum

Inside the house, a pendulum marks perfect time pristine
slashing with shadows that bisect ground and overhead light,

stain the floor like charcoal smudging prints along
the oriental rug continually contracting into themselves,

absorb into fibers synthesized, reemerging 60 times again.
I ignore the bar and let my eyes swing in shifting rhythms

with perpetual slices into light that beats onto surfaces
reflecting off, and I listen to hours in cyclical repetition

starting at some unknown point in the room that extends
into corners. Inside, I catalog hours into night

with recycled increments, and I'm lulled to sleep by ticks
of spring and fall equinox again as they eclipse my carpet.

IV. Constellation Horologium

Between his finger and the stars, La Caille drew onto
space, marking shifting lines that move with precision

navigated through metallic moons, divided
the sky with quadrants and mythological stick figures.

He reclaimed etchings, notched Huygens'
pendulum with the smudge of his finger

over his telescopic eyepiece. He stayed inside
the shadows marking the hours by movements of stars.

I watch the night sky for a swinging arm, anything
to mark the passage of time as I wade through black grass

and occasional periods of artificial lights.

3.) Hand Carvings in Mensa

Today, I found two handprints
while sand-digging beneath earth layers:

one fossilized by the rhythmic ocean,
the other mirrored from a point

miles above sea level, not as far from
the sky, with lines raised like feathers
running across the palm-shaped hole.

I found fingers next, placing mine inside
yours, rock into mud again from the

heat of the sun or the friction of my hand,
and I am holding on to yours again or first;

I can't remember anymore. Your hands were
large enough to blot out the day behind one

convex palm and press fingers together into
gaps that disappear with the beach before sunset.

At night, you liked to stand so close to the sky
and the cold rock that frigidly reflects the sunlight.

I want to look for prints in the moon or just palm
lines traced between the stars, but it's the sun

that rises too early, sets too late for images to
harden in the absence of sun heat. Instead, I

look for hemispheres intersecting in the ground
as you flex open and shut the center of your hand.

4.) Argo Navis: The Journey From

I. Puppis

I can see you in the morning, small between archaic
alphabetic symbols, mapping lines between letters
into words. You're drinking coffee, and periodically
lost in black sky reflections solidified within the rim.

Tangled in string, you've webbed yourself into
dead languages, tracing the Aramaic symbols
you've never been able to pronounce in the first place.
Rotating them around each other until they become

a Greek Bible, and you're authoring these new fables
from words intended to betray their own mythology.
Someday, they'll sit stagnant in later translations pressed
in hotel drawers by the Gideons. You don't know this;

you've got your coffee-black dreams where you rename
those foreign tongues in pictures because there aren't
phonemes in images, only the impression. Rip out
the pages and fold them into sculptures of boats and birds.

You sleep alone on these pages, connecting in solitude
the letters with crucifixes and snakes holding them in.
These are the real stories: the misshapen stars bleeding

ink through the pages.

Several ancient civilizations recognized the ship in the Argo Navis constellation, at one time the largest constellation in the sky, before La Caille, finding it too enormous to study effectively, broke the constellation into three parts — Carina (keel or hull), Puppis (poop deck or stern), and Vela (sails) — in 1752. The full Argo is drawn here by Johannes Hevelius (1611-1687).

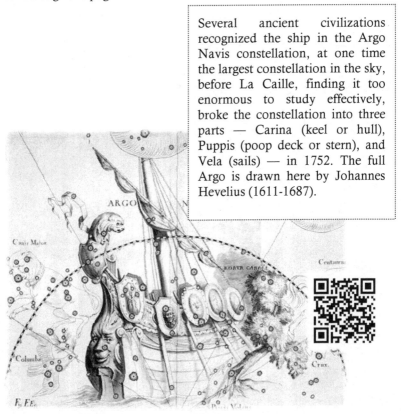

II. Pyrix

You're always logical when it comes to day—
live at night under the atmosphere and humid clouds.
Dream silent in film stills and travel south,
drawing the maps before you sleep at sunrise.

You couldn't deconstruct your father into something
foreign in daylight translations, black and white in
metrical numerics. You wanted to measure the arc
of each bone, to learn him in a more sterile language.

But this isn't the story of your dreams. You don't
duplicate him on the Southern sky. Instead, you sail
down, cut through thick earth behind you with
hemispheres and equators that stretch around.

You pass through every season as you reinvent the
globe's dimensions. You're bleeding ships and other
scientific myths out from the otherwise opaque sky,

stars patterned into stories. You never knew you wrote
the Proverbs sailors recite on clear nights, chanting
proper names and angles as prayers for home or a destination.

III. Carina

In nightmares, crack through surface into breast
bone, sift through the charred remnants until
you reach arteries and the heart in oxygen shock.

The lines inside were pre-drawn with folds of wet
muscle, greased fat-pocketed shadows, wrapped tight
around the arteries.

So many others, greens turn to gray, and the
shadows disappear in one tone as you try to
keep coloring his sleeping cheeks. Your hot hands caving in
the places where he's already dead. And while atoms cold
fall from fingers, you draw imaginary lines, trying to constellate
him in one living piece.

His heart will disperse through limp veins; it'll dangle and
spill over the now-rigid spinal cord. The dead skin merges with
clean air, and you can't trace perfect circles with a blade
in his chest. But you note that his bile bleeds in geometric
figures with a pivoting scalpel jointed with stars.

IV. Vela

So instead, you position yourself
so far south of
north, south of
language, false theologies.
Filtered through telescopic views
and mathematical data, you
now speak with no nightmares.

I watch in awe as you construct
ships, weave the sails that will carry
     the journey from
     to search for
        south.

You'll populate this new sky with
myths scrawled in celestial
hieroglyphics. Draw yourself
that island; catch the wind that
draws you into the eye of
        any tropical storm.

La Caille's Southern
Planisphere Map:
dated 1752.

PLANISPHERE des Étoiles Australes

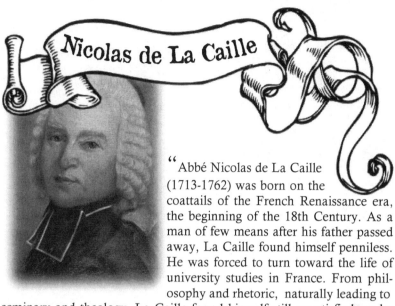

Nicolas de La Caille

"Abbé Nicolas de La Caille (1713-1762) was born on the coattails of the French Renaissance era, the beginning of the 18th Century. As a man of few means after his father passed away, La Caille found himself penniless. He was forced to turn toward the life of university studies in France. From philosophy and rhetoric, naturally leading to seminary and theology, La Caille found himself still unsatisfied, so he began the pursuit of physics and astronomy. Abruptly, after earning the church rank of Abbé, he then quit and left the Northern Hemisphere for the Southern. At the Cape of Good Hope, he successfully cataloged over 10,000 Southern stars, found 42 nebulous objects, and he personally observed, predicted, and named Haley's Comet. In the process of cataloging stars, La Caille named 14 new constellations, and at times, reappropriated stars from preexisting constellations if he felt the mythology had been lost. Instead, he replaced the classical stories with scientific and mathematical tools, quoting, most likely in French, that math and science are at the root of any good art. The more I've read about him, the more I've fallen in love with his story. Plus, he has his own crater on the moon."

—*Angie Jeffreys Schomp*

5.) Dreams of Sex in Other Hemispheres

I dream of warm blood, lapsed against mine,
under the sheets with steam and the
things that go with it. I'm printed against
the cotton patterned purple or blue
across the mattress, beneath your breath.

I watch your pear-like eyes, I see black pearls
somewhere south of here; you're foreign in
another hemisphere again. You can't hear me

51

over your tropical storm: all your nightmares gusting inland
at you—you think from me. I can't brush the wet hair from
your brow. Instead, you invent the geometry of us, shapes
pressed in the shadowy fabric. You predict your impact
against the way your leg tangles with my arm. I am your

mathematical equation, my body mapped, manipulated
into graphs. Gravity drips a blurry pen, and I disappear
within the parallax of your closed lids on other coasts.

6.) Astronomy of Body

Scoring lines into navy soft between lighted
freckles with mythological mathematics,
you calligraphically engraved the sky by night.

I like the way you press your fingers firmly in my skin,
navy blots of sky rub off onto pale stomach. I was
born without birthmarks: you've carved them in.

It's easier to let bone become soft,
melt into fabric, so I land peacefully

against the resistant wall. Joints of your index
finger continually pressing through my right cheek.

Navigating your body onto my stars, I gaze out
at the Southern sky as you embed your map in mine:

scrawled lines over a photo of leftover stars, or me;
you say you made me a sculptor's tool.

7.) Stars Caught in the River

Sun rises over five fingers burning the stars out,
hot light magnified through morning clouds that
hang wet and low. The moon slides off to the east or
south, and you can't bear to touch my skin hot from day.
I'm not a myth for you to trace anymore.

I'm no goddess pointed with stars cut out from the sky
that somehow subtract the miles between us. You've
only shadowed my face with bruises in the night. I'm not
the sand sculptures you built at noon, eager for sundown.

As you take your hand to shield the light from your eyes,
you leave mine exposed and tell me the story of Phaethon,
slipping into the Greek for the places you don't want me to
understand.

But I know nothing about your mythology or the physics of
stealing stars from water. You say you left his body or mine
burning in the shallow end of the river, flames pooling at
the bank. All you feel is your fingers blistering when they're
too close to the sun.

8.) Reticulum

The summer sun falls down behind a hemisphere;
stars stick to night like it's flypaper. I watch them
swarm as I shift my thighs away from the suction

of the plastic lawn chair on Wild Magnolia's patio.
We're outside with the Christmas tree lights
illuminating August, wrapped around the wooden fence.

Loose Blues blow hot on my neck and sweat dried there
about an hour or two margaritas ago. It's open mic indoors
where some people will never truly understand the
growl of a saxophone. The others flail to inaudible melodies.

I recenter by staring up to focus—you said astronomers use
crosshairs of a telescopic lens to locate themselves inside
the netted grid. Tequila, green like absinthe, reflects away from
you: ice knocks the glass sides. Lime juice ferments on my
tongue. I focus

on the dim stars and the salt burning as I recall the crosshairs
I found left behind in an autumn sky where I rename you with her
name. If we look close, we will redraw our tempos on a summer sky.

The Ballad of
Augustin Lefavre

R. JOSEPH CAPET

A fell wind rifled the barley, unharvested and high,
which swayed in the starlit field, teasing the lavender sky.
The scent of the last blooms of summer o'er France still lazily
    hung;
the men lay asleep in the trenches, where the Marseillaise had
    been sung.
The moon settled light on a cloud, like a leaf upon the moor.
Augustin Lefavre dreamt of times before the war
when he'd heard Debussy in the concert hall in Lyons years
    before.

Now 'twas Wagner's shrieking shells that pierced the autumn
    air,
the machine gun pizzicato's bombastic Teuton flair
that echoed through the chilling wind of autumn's mute
    Ardennes
as Augustin Lefavre, with collar turned, sat nursing his
    fountain pen.

He searched his mind for photographs of that long-lost summer's eve,
when Corinne's hair shone 'neath the moon like the petals of the trees—
when her sacred laugh had echoed 'round the bells of the silent church,
and the nightingale had sung her praise from its lofty, hidden perch.

He grasped for ethereal verses that this image could contain.
He sought th'unspeakable patter of the pelting winter rain.
He longed for that delicate couplet that at the start of his sonnet
    belonged.
He wanted to write a poem like Debussy wrote his songs.

But the paper he held was stained with ink in jagged little rows
and torn at the end of every line by the pen's ferocious blows.
The meter matched the quickened pace of shells crashing in fallen leaves
or the sonorous roll of the thundering hooves of the valkyries' chosen
    steeds.

His eyes raked the verses before him as he read them aloud to the east.
His pulse beat aloud in his forehead long after his reading had ceased.
With a twitch all his fingers contracted; the poem fell fast to the ground.
A Sopwith some three miles distant was the darkening night's only
    sound.

He raised up the torn scrap of paper as a necromancer the slain
and turned to each line of his writing to ask of each line whence it came,
but none would betray its creator, each stood defiantly bold,
and he knew that this Teutonic paean had come from his own Gallic
    soul.

He read over again the beginning, like the drums of a tribal chief,
with their low and monotonous echo, their menacing primitive beat.
This was not the delicate couplet that at the start of his sonnet belonged.
He was trying to write a poem like Debussy wrote his songs.

So Augustin scratched out the alien rhymes that had flowed from his
    treacherous hand
and marshaled once more what muses he had arrayed at his command.
He conjured forth the holy space of that grand and gilded room
where he'd last heard tumble off the keys the strains of *Clair de Lune*.

Then he touched pen to paper and watched the black ink flow
like oil from the armored engines rumbling down below,
and there, where his vowels should have sung like a fawn in the
    afternoon,
the consonants of an alien tongue chanted Tannhäuser's baleful tune.

He struck through the lines with a flourish, filled with a terrible fright.
The black ink sprayed forth like the vapor that came to the trenches at
    night.
On autumn's still, shivering field he desperately sought the sound
that served as his Persean shield to modernity's funeral mound.

But then the overture from Faust descended through the pass,
like an evening mist to crystallize upon each blade of grass.
The darkened notes entwined themselves 'round dandelion stems
and let loose their seeds to take their flight from out the doomed
    Ardennes.

With foreign thoughts he slid his hand down to the pistol butt
and cocked the hammer gracefully, keeping one eye shut.
There was no delicate couplet that to this great saga belonged
and he would never write a poem like Debussy wrote his songs.

Antoine-Joseph Gorsas

"While reading Nicholas Roe's *Wordsworth and Coleridge: The Radical Years*, I was struck by a passage about one supposed interaction between William Wordsworth and Thomas Carlyle. In his book, *Reminiscences*, Carlyle maintains that Wordsworth told him, at a dinner party they both attended around 1840, that he'd witnessed the guillotining of Antoine-Joseph Gorsas in October 1793. Roe is not the only historian to write of that section in Carlyle's late-in-life book. The consensus, however, is that there is a lack of evidence indicating Wordsworth ever made such a trip into France in the fall of 1793. Roe writes, in describing Carlyle's reference to the story: "Perhaps Carlyle's recollection should be taken as an imaginative truth, in which case Wordsworth's shadowy presence at the scaffold was not only as appalled spectator but simultaneously as victim and as executioner, too."[1] This effort in narrative nonfiction, then, is a description of "imaginative truth," regarding that probably-apocryphal detail about Wordsworth, and Gorsas' sudden end. The piece is set in March 1841, in London, extrapolating a timeframe from Carlyle's writing. It is my hope the research into pertinent details of Wordsworth and Carlyle in that period—modest as the effort proves in light of what *could* be done in such a narrative fleshing-out—is sufficient to summon a convincing picture of Roe's "imaginative truth," and that the reader will forgive a minimum of injected particulars in connection with what might have been served for supper or what the party imbibed that evening.[2]"

—*James O'Brien*

[1] See Nicholas Roe, *Wordsworth and Coleridge: The Radical Years* (Oxford: Clarendon Press, 1988): 41.

[2] All such details, however, are culled from foods Wordsworth seems to prefer in Dorothy Wordsworth, *The Grasmere Journals* (Oxford: Clarendon Press, 1991).

Gorsas' Guillotine: A Nonfiction Narrative of Wordsworth and Carlyle

JAMES O'BRIEN

homas Carlyle was expounding his book, the one opposing certain economic theories held by certain English liberals, that much was clear; the man's voice cut the din.[1] William Wordsworth turned his fork and cut his pork, and answered Spedding's thought on Francis Bacon. Spedding seemed obsessed with the man, tonight. Wordsworth thought of Spedding as a man displaced, out of gainful work for adhering to his principles. Which was a good enough reason to be out of work, in any case. Natural, perhaps, that Spedding would gravitate to philosophies of duty and ethics—Bacon, or anyone else for that matter.[2] But it was Bacon.

While Spedding spoke, Wordsworth's eyes wandered to the outside wall, where afternoon faded from the windows. It was a sharp air, out there, still a winter's air despite the lateness of March. He thought of the coach ride from the north, from Ambleside.[3] Down to

---

[1] This exercise in narrative nonfiction is set in London in early 1841, about one year after Thomas Carlyle published *Chartism* (December 1839), his treatise on poverty, the poor, justice, and the English economic system. His passion for the work ran high, though getting the words into print involved some struggle on his part. It sold briskly, however, rattling English liberals, who found Carlyle's criticism of their economic theories unorthodox. Given the minor uproar he'd created, it is conceivable Carlyle would be asked about and would speak of the book at dinner parties during the year that followed. See James Anthony Froude, *Thomas Carlyle: A History of His Life in London, 1834-1881* (St. Claire Shores, Mi.: Scholarly Press, 1970): 182-186.

[2] Wordsworth is speaking to James Spedding, recorded present at least once at a party also attended by Wordsworth. See Thomas Carlyle, *Reminiscences* (London and New York: J. M. Dent and E. P. Dutton, 1932): 300. Spedding, a scholar and writer, was, in early 1841, ending—or just about to end—his work with the colonial office. He would soon start a 30-year project of editing the work of Francis Bacon. See Leslie Stephen, "Spedding, James (1808–1881)," rev. W. A. Sessions, in *Oxford Dictionary of National Biography*, ed. H. C. G. Matthew and Brian Harrison (Oxford: Oxford University Press, 2004); online ed., ed. Lawrence Goldman, May 2006, http://oxforddnb.com/view/article/26090 (accessed October 20, 2009).

[3] In 1841, Wordsworth lived in Ambleside, near to Grasmere. There was some promotion in that year of Wordsworth as a candidate for poet laureate by theologian, Frederick William Faber. It is conceivable that Faber would arrange for gatherings of the authors

the city, with lunches on the first day in Preston, on the second in Northampton. The overnight had been in Birmingham, where the bed at the inn looked more comfortable than it proved. That made for a long morning, and this afternoon there had been Faber, with whom he had to visit in London, and with whom he'd be asked to sit again, he imagined, before he could return to Ambleside. It was a whole business, this back and forth to talk of Oxford and laureates; it was Faber's irritation, particularly. Wordsworth's back hurt; the return ride threatened piles.[4] Still, Faber, in all his agitation, was easier on the ears than a room full of writers and their rum. It wasn't the rum he disliked, anyway. Someone laughed at Carlyle, and there followed much clapping of backs. Wordsworth finished the tail ends on his plate, moving around what he didn't want. The peas weren't very fresh at all.

Later, for whatever reason, he found himself once again gravitating to Carlyle. Or Carlyle to him, as the formula worked out. Wordsworth took the corner spot first, and so here the man came for more discourse.[5] He imagined Carlyle liked to hear him talk, and despite his earlier audience, Carlyle did seem, at these times, inclined to listen, as well as speak. Before, at dinners like these, they'd talked of poets, and issues generally English. Tonight, with the soreness in him, and the general weariness, Wordsworth worried he'd wax darkly with his corner companion. Perhaps he should give him fair warning. Didn't Carlyle deserve a warning? Carlyle, for all his good reminiscences of the past—the orange tincture of the fire on his cheeks—far enough from the crush, but not too far from the fat black bottles of rum?

It had been a morning party at some other tavern, maybe on St. James's—their first real conversation.[6] Wordsworth had been in good spirits, that day, and talk of literature and poems and people had turned around and around, and that was the first day he'd really taken notice of

---

and academic elite around Oxford and London to press his candidate into the minds of others. Wordsworth ultimately took the title in 1843, following the death of Robert Southey. See Stephen Gill, "Wordsworth, William (1770–1850)," in *Oxford Dictionary of National Biography*, ed. H. C. G. Matthew and Brian Harrison (Oxford: Oxford University Press, 2004); online ed., ed. Lawrence Goldman, January 2008, http://oxforddnb.com/view/article/29973 (accessed October 20, 2009).

[4] There is some precedent for such an affliction within the spectrum of Wordsworth's various lifelong physical complaints. See Dorothy Wordsworth, *The Grasmere Journals* (Oxford: Clarendon Press, 1991): 30.

[5] Carlyle remarks on Wordsworth's tendency to stay clear of the noisy middle of a party: "He was willing to talk with me in a corner, in noisy extensive circles; having weak eyes, and little loving the general babble current in such place." See Thomas Carlyle, *Reminiscences*: 302.

[6] As for the year of their first meeting, there is some discrepancy. Carlyle writes: "It was perhaps about 1840 that I first had any decisive meeting with Wordsworth, or made any really personal acquaintance with him," and he goes on to describe the first substantive conversation between the two at an unnamed tavern on "St. James's Street." In a footnote to this assertion, however, C. E. Norton notes that Carlyle made an entry in his *Journal*, on June 1, 1836, that he'd "seen Wordsworth again." See Carlyle, *Reminiscences*: 299, 299n.

Carlyle. Over the months since, at dinner parties and suppers (more than one of them called by Faber, or involving Faber, persistent Faber), when Carlyle appeared, Wordsworth had felt some compulsion to draw him near, to ask the man his thoughts on this matter or that matter; he had liked the man's *French Revolution*, in the first place.[7] And here he came again, only Wordsworth wished he brought with him cups of the rum, but they'd both neglected such details, in breaking away.

"Not a slight cast, these characters," said Carlyle. "Good men, these, do you think, William?"

"I think they are fine men, some of them, and most of them useful," Wordsworth said. "Although, if we are to talk of good men, I say it is in struggle against great odds toward which I considerably weight my evaluation; it is not always this pleasant conversation over pork and peas."

Carlyle let him go on, and not long into it, as Wordsworth suspected from the start, the Revolution rose between them: the Assembly, the Girondins, and the Mountain. He spoke of Godwin, and the island of thought for Wordsworth that Godwin's writing made in the months of blood that followed those first hopeful celebrations in Calais.[8]

"Do I speak too freely?" Wordsworth asked. He really rather would have had some rum, then. "We all spoke freely, in those days, and some of us to our later regret."[9]

Carlyle waved a white-shirted server toward them, and soon a cup of the rum was produced. Wordsworth knew what questions would follow, given that he'd broached certain subjects, and he let Carlyle take his course, as he took the cup proffered. The liquid stung his tongue and sizzled the back of his throat. He deflected Carlyle, in part, speaking instead of the *Courier*, and then of Gorsas.[10]

"Do you mean that you knew him?" Carlyle asked.

---

[7] Carlyle had written a history of the war: *The French Revolution* (1837).

[8] Wordsworth visited Calais on July 13, 1790, witnessing the celebration of the first anniversary of the Revolution. It moved him, and he wrote about it in Book Six of *The Prelude*: "How bright a face is worn when joy of one/Is joy of tens of millions." See Nicholas Roe, *Wordsworth and Coleridge: The Radical Years* (Oxford: Clarendon Press, 1988): 20.

[9] A bit of license taken here. It is clear, however, that Wordsworth's initial support and enthusiasm for ideas of parliamentary reform (Godwin's *Political Justice*, for example) and his support of the French Revolution at its outset, became an issue with which both he and his likeminded community, including Samuel Taylor Coleridge, would have to grapple as the violence in France became acute, come 1793. Coleridge did so on the page, in letters of 1803, for example, in which he denied connections to "any party or club or society." Wordsworth responded by somewhat sublimating his feelings about France's transformation between 1789 and 1793, obscuring portions of his history of involvement with politics, reformists, and Revolutionary France in Book Ten of *The Prelude*. See Roe, *Wordsworth and Coleridge: The Radical Years*: 3-7.

[10] Antoine-Joseph Gorsas, French politician and dissident, who in 1792, published a newspaper, the *Courier*, in connection with the French Revolution. See Hugh Gough, *The Newspaper Press in the French Revolution* (Chicago: Dorsey Press, 1988): 91.

For a moment, Wordsworth let the inquiry linger. In the ruddy haze of the fireplace, Carlyle's face was suffuse with contrast. It seemed to shift as he dipped his head slightly, sipping from his cup.

"I knew this man," Wordsworth said, at last.[11]

"How did the news of the end, then, come to you?"

Wordsworth again lifted his cup; the twinge in his back seemed wrapped now in warm and layered gauze. "He was the first *deputy* sent to the scaffold. And this was a thunderhead, Carlyle. Or like a mist of some ominous quality, coursing the same bricks along which we had happily rushed. But where were the French flowered arches, now? Baskets of horror, instead, and a different bloom of rose. The word spread."[12]

"Do you mean that you were there, William?" Carlyle asked. "For I have never heard of this, a public sentiment, such spread of news."[13]

"Where will it *end*, when you have set an example in *this* kind?" Wordsworth said.[14] "So it was, the end of Gorsas; not so very long ago, it seems to me, tonight."

Carlyle pressed him for more, wanting the details of the days around it, wanting to be certain on the point: Had Wordsworth set foot again on French soil in 1793? Had he seen the lead-gray blade under the bruised bowl of that October afternoon?[15] Wordsworth felt Carlyle's urgency, but how to steer him to the main point? Not whether he had been there on any particular day; rather they had all set ink to page in the days before the sails appeared on the Scheldt, before Louis' end in that awful mid-sentence of the scaffold.[16] They had set ink to page again

---

[11] In a volume from Wordsworth's library, Adam Sisman writes, "There is a marginal note where Gorsas is mentioned: 'I knew this man. W. W.'" See Adam Sisman, *The Friendship: Wordsworth and Coleridge* (New York: Penguin Viking, 2007): 58.

[12] Carlyle wrote of this part of the conversation: "He had been in France in the earlier or secondary stage of the Revolution; had witnessed the struggle of *Girondins* and *Mountain*, in particular the execution of Gorsas, 'the first *Deputy* sent to the Scaffold,' and testified strongly to the ominous feeling which that event produced in everybody, and of which he himself still seemed to retain something: 'Where will it *end*, when you have set an example in *this* kind?'" Emphases are Carlyle's. See Carlyle, *Reminiscences*: 303.

[13] In *Reminiscences*, Carlyle notes his surprise at Wordsworth's details about the "ominous feeling which that event produced in everybody." The passage reads: "I knew well about Gorsas; but had found, in my readings, no trace of the public emotion his death excited." See Carlyle, *Reminiscences*: 303.

[14] See Carlyle, *Reminiscences*: 303.

[15] Gorsas was executed on October 7, 1793. See Kenneth Johnston, *The Hidden Wordsworth* (New York: W. W. Norton, 1998): 279.

[16] Several historical details in a row, here: In December 1792, French ships sailed the River Scheldt, a waterway shared by northern France, Belgium, and the Netherlands. In doing so, the Prussians deemed a British-Prussian treaty forbidding international trade in those waters violated, and the pressure on England to react to the French intensified. The French guillotined Louis XVI in January 1793. The French ambassador was dismissed, and the British government from then on considered itself at war with France. See Roe, *Wordsworth and Coleridge: The Radical Years*: 120.

afterward, too, but they had suffered little for it—he and Coleridge and others—while another man certainly wanted for the poet's shield.[17]

"What do you think of Spedding?" Wordsworth asked, of a sudden.[18] The two of them stopped, then, for a moment. A single log, round and thick as a man's arm, shifted atop the stack in the hearth, halfway across the room from them. A white-shirted boy took their cups. Perhaps there would be other cups. Perhaps Faber would make his entrance, soon. It was the end of a long day for an old man of seventy.[19]

James Spedding

[For further reading, please see James O'Brien's bibliography on the Acknowledgments page in the back of this journal.]

---

[17] In another moment of license on my part, Wordsworth is thinking here about the harsh treatment by the British government of some reformist writers of the early 1790s, such as Thomas Paine, who was found guilty of seditious libel in 1792 for such monographs as *The Rights of Man*. He compares, in his mind, Paine's lot to his own experience of dissidence, in the role of poet. See Roe, *Wordsworth and Coleridge: The Radical Years*: 118-119.

[18] Following his utterance about Gorsas, according to Carlyle, Wordsworth would say nothing more substantial about the story. They soon switched topics, Carlyle writes. See Carlyle, *Reminiscences*: 303.

[19] The story is set prior to Wordsworth's birthday on April 7. He would turn 71 in the spring of 1841.

I wandered lonely as a cloud

I wandered lonely as a cloud
That floats on high o'er vales and hills,
When all at once I saw a crowd,
A host, of golden daffodils;
Beside the lake, beneath the trees,
Fluttering and dancing in the breeze.

Continuous as the stars that shine
And twinkle on the milky way,
They stretched in never-ending line
Along the margin of a bay:
Ten thousand saw I at a glance,
Tossing their heads in sprightly dance.

The waves beside them danced; but they
Outdid the sparkling waves in glee:
A poet could not but be gay,
In such a jocund company:
I gazed—and gazed—but little thought
What wealth the show to me had brought:

For oft, when on my couch I lie
In vacant or in pensive mood,
They flash upon that inward eye
Which is the bliss of solitude;
And then my heart with pleasure fills,
And dances with the daffodils.

The world is too much with us

The world is too much with us; late and soon,
Getting and spending, we lay waste our powers:
Little we see in Nature that is ours;
We have given our hearts away, a sordid boon!
This Sea that bares her bosom to the moon;
The winds that will be howling at all hours,
And are up-gathered now like sleeping flowers;
For this, for everything, we are out of tune;
It moves us not. Great God! I'd rather be
A Pagan suckled in a creed outworn;
So might I, standing on this pleasant lea,
Have glimpses that would make me less forlorn;
Have sight of Proteus rising from the sea;
Or hear old Triton blow his wreathèd horn.

WILLIAM WORDSWORTH

William Wordsworth

France, an Ode

SAMUEL T. COLERIDGE, 1772-1834

I.

Ye Clouds! that far above me float and pause,
Whose pathless march no mortal may control!
Ye Ocean-Waves! that, wheresoe'er ye roll,
Yield homage only to eternal laws!
Ye Woods! that listen to the night-birds singing,
Midway the smooth and perilous slope reclined.
Save when your own imperious branches swinging,
Have made a solemn music of the wind!
Where, like a man beloved of God,
Through glooms, which never woodman trod,
How oft, pursuing fancies holy,
My moonlight way o'er flowering weeds I wound,
Inspired, beyond the guess of folly,
By each rude shape and wild unconquerable sound!
O ye loud Waves! and O ye Forests high!
And O ye Clouds that far above me soared!
Thou rising Sun! thou blue rejoicing Sky!
Yea, every thing that is and will be free!
Bear witness for me, wheresoe'er ye be,
With what deep worship I have still adored
The spirit of divinest Liberty.

II.

When France in wrath her giant-limbs upreared,
And with that oath, which smote air, earth, and sea,
Stamped her strong foot and said she would be free,
Bear witness for me, how I hoped and feared!
With what a joy my lofty gratulation
Unawed I sang, amid a slavish band:
And when to whelm the disenchanted nation,
Like fiends embattled by a wizard's wand,
The Monarchs marched in evil day,
And Britain joined the dire array;
Though dear her shores and circling ocean,
Though many friendships, many youthful loves
Had swoln the patriot emotion
And flung a magic light o'er all her hills and groves;
Yet still my voice, unaltered, sang defeat
To all that braved the tyrant-quelling lance,

And shame too long delayed and vain retreat!
For ne'er, O Liberty! with partial aim
I dimmed thy light or damped thy holy flame;
But blessed the paeans of delivered France,
And hung my head and wept at Britain's name.

III.

"And what," I said, "though Blasphemy's loud scream
With that sweet music of deliverance strove!
Though all the fierce and drunken passions wove
A dance more wild than e'er was maniac's dream!
Ye storms, that round the dawning East assembled,
The Sun was rising, though ye hid his light!"
And when, to soothe my soul, that hoped and trembled,
The dissonance ceased, and all seemed calm and bright;
When France her front deep-scarr'd and gory
Concealed with clustering wreaths of glory;
When, insupportably advancing,
Her arm made mockery of the warrior's ramp;
While timid looks of fury glancing,
Domestic treason, crushed beneath her fatal stamp,
Writhed like a wounded dragon in his gore;
Then I reproached my fears that would not flee;
"And soon," I said, "shall Wisdom teach her lore
In the low huts of them that toil and groan!
And, conquering by her happiness alone,
Shall France compel the nations to be free,
Till Love and Joy look round, and call the Earth their own."

IV.

Forgive me, Freedom! O forgive those dreams!
I hear thy voice, I hear thy loud lament,
From bleak Helvetia's icy caverns sent—
I hear thy groans upon her blood-stained streams!
Heroes, that for your peaceful country perished,
And ye that, fleeing, spot your mountain-snows
With bleeding wounds; forgive me, that I cherished
One thought that ever blessed your cruel foes!
To scatter rage, and traitorous guilt,
Where Peace her jealous home had built;
A patriot-race to disinherit
Of all that made their stormy wilds so dear;
And with inexpiable spirit
To taint the bloodless freedom of the mountaineer—
O France, that mockest Heaven, adulterous, blind,

And patriot only in pernicious toils!
Are these thy boasts, Champion of human kind?
To mix with Kings in the low lust of sway,
Yell in the hunt, and share the murderous prey;
To insult the shrine of Liberty with spoils
From freemen torn; to tempt and to betray?

V.

The Sensual and the Dark rebel in vain,
Slaves by their own compulsion! In mad game
They burst their manacles and wear the name
Of Freedom, graven on a heavier chain!
O Liberty! with profitless endeavor
Have I pursued thee, many a weary hour;
But thou nor swell'st the victor's strain, nor ever
Didst breathe thy soul in forms of human power.
Alike from all, howe'er they praise thee,
(Nor prayer, nor boastful name delays thee)
Alike from Priestcraft's harpy minions,
And factious Blasphemy's obscener slaves,
Thou speedest on thy subtle pinions,
The guide of homeless winds, and playmate of the waves!
And there I felt thee!—on that sea-cliff's verge,
Whose pines, scarce traveled by the breeze above,
Had made one murmur with the distant surge!
Yes, while I stood and gazed, my temples bare,
And shot my being through earth, sea, and air,
Possessing all things with intensest love,
O Liberty! my spirit felt thee there.

Samuel Coleridge

Cui Bono

What is Hope? A smiling rainbow
Children follow through the wet;
'Tis not here, still yonder, yonder:
Never urchin found it yet.

What is Life? A thawing iceboard
On a sea with sunny shore;—
Gay we sail; it melts beneath us;
We are sunk, and seen no more.

What is Man? A foolish baby,
Vainly strives, and fights, and frets;
Demanding all, deserving nothing;—
One small grave is what he gets.

THOMAS CARLYLE, 1795-1881

Thomas Carlyle

FEATURED WRITER

A. Jay Adler

A. Jay Adler, a New Yorker always, is Professor of English, Emeritus at LA SW College. He earned his BA, with concentrations in English lit, philosophy, and film at City University of NY, and his MA and MPhil degrees in English literature from Columbia University. Earlier careers were as an executive in the air courier industry and as a troubled soul. (The troubles passed, but the soul remains a lifelong challenge.) In the courier business, Adler directed client shipments and himself to points around the globe. Along with writing, literature, film, jazz, photography, thinking, and general adventure, travel—by air, sea, locomotive, cable, four wheels, two wheels (motorized and muscle-driven), and by foot—remains a passion.

The former poetry editor for the now-defunct *West* magazine, Adler writes in various genres of fiction, nonfiction, and poetry and has written for the theater and won awards for screenwriting. Academic specializations include: British and American Modernism, the novel, James Joyce studies, rhetoric and composition, argumentation, and critical thinking. Adler's blog, *the sad red earth,* is one venue for his political and cultural commentary, where he pays special attention to the analysis of arguments.

A 1989 interviewee for a junior fellowship in the Harvard Society of Fellows, Adler was awarded a 2002 residency grant in poetry from the Vermont Studio Center. Among several screenplays, *What We Were Thinking Of* has won several awards, including second prize at the 1998 Maui Writers Conference Screenwriting Competition. During his 2008-09 sabbatical year, Adler traveled the country by motor home, documenting Native American life. Adler's article, "Aboriginal Sin," was included in the anthology, *Global Viewpoints: Indigenous Peoples*, from Greenhaven Press.

The Cemeteries at Père-Lachaise and Montparnasse

A. JAY ADLER

Samuel Beckett waits the wasting changes here,
lies, to my surprise, in an earthly grave.
In what grave sense does he remain, then, and not go?
And Baudelaire is here, and Balzac, and Hugo:
all the flares that burst and flickered,
embered into monuments of fame and stone.

Beauvoir shares the plot and stone with Sartre,
though they would not split the rent and gas in life:
they have no need for their own space now
in the cold autonomy of the dark and silent.

A spare "MD" engraved in granite
marks the last *écriture de* Duras,
and where Morrison burned and crashed to rest,
his fans leave lyrics that urge their human voice
to "break on through" to some other side.

And wild as Wilde lived his life,
he's Wilder still in death: an unknown benefactress
restores his tomb, where scores of rosy lipstick lips
kiss in swirls of renewed delight
his latest marble monument.

They all appear where I least expect them—
there in the solid ground, now
in the living light of an autumn day.
Tristan Tzara, just one letter in a random
alphabet along a shaded walk, da da.
Man Ray, Seyrig, Sarah Bernhardt,
in their quiet places, Simone Signoret
and Yves Montand in endless embrace again,
die and depart and drift
into aging pages of repetition and renown,
dwell among the sacred scenes and bookmarks in midnight light
—die and depart and reassert their natural selves
before each mortal, passing gaze,
beside each set of scraping soles.

So their light lingers, headlights in a fog,
but they leave their darkness, too,
as if the spirit's voyage requires a body's anchor
or where might they be found, or how afraid to leave?
And Eugène Ionescu hopes that Christ awaits him.

Turn by turn, far corner by corner,
I find them oddly still in the world of dreams and fears,
and I save for the end Alfred Dreyfus—
most unexpected, most lonely,
farthest from any marker on a map.
Crooked aisle by aisle, angled row by row,
I scan the names and lives, but the soldier is sentenced
unjustly again: I cannot find him.

The gnarled and bony-fingered branches
splay leafless against the drear October sky,
and what is there and isn't there
hangs nowhere in the cemetery air.
It is Paris 2003, or 4 or 5,
and there are the family come to visit,
the unknown lover who stands alone,
an open gate, the nearby traffic,
the fresh and wilting bounty of Serge Gainsbourg's tributes
the mausolea, the hidden reaches,
the statues, and a child running
(Samuel Beckett waiting)
a cold stone bench, the hand that writes,
the blown leaf, the millipede,
the shadows of them all.

Twenty-Five Hundred Years before 9/11: Van Gogh's Eyes

Before my drive to Normandy and my second stay in Paris, I had left Julia in St. Rémy-de-Provence, where she taught a photo workshop to the eight students who had braved their fears to fly there less than two weeks after 9/11. I stayed a few days myself before leaving and did some historical and artistic touring. Along one of the primary spoke roads that leads to the center of St. Rémy, about a mile out, are the ruins of the ancient town of Glanum. Dating back over twenty-five hundred years, Glanum was settled by the Saylens, a Celto-Ligurian tribe, and evolved, after conquest, over subsequent Greek and Roman eras. Though, except for a couple of monuments, the town was long covered over by soil and time, its entire foundation has now been unearthed, as well as some nearly whole structures.

Throughout the preceding month, I had engaged, amid my travels, in much historical re-imagining, imagining soon to be concentrated by circumstance. At one point, then, as I walked the ruins of Glanum, I chose to descend the winding stairs that led to the once-sacred waters of an underground stream. I stood and tried to inhabit the sense of life that would have accompanied the bare feet dipped hopefully into the now fetid water I declined to enter. What, I wondered, was the wholeness of that world, the totality of that belief unconcerned to justify itself through reason, beyond reason, at once at home with itself, in complete conviction, yet sufficiently agitated by its contrary to seek to destroy it. For, though they were a spiritual people, the Glanic people were also a war-like people, and the frieze around the town's intact Mausolée and monument to its dead enshrines, with faces worn away by time but with vividness and vitality, the fierceness and slaughter of battle. I try to imagine that, too.

Very near Glanum, across a field, is the thousand-year-old Saint-Paul monastery, the asylum where Vincent Van Gogh sought care after cutting off his ear in 1888. "I do not hide from you the fact that I would rather have died than cause or suffer so much unhappiness," Van Gogh wrote to his brother, Theo, before entering Saint-Paul. Van Gogh stayed at Saint-Paul for just over a year. Although he suffered several incapacitating depressions during his time there, he managed to produce over a hundred and fifty paintings, many of them among his greatest and most famous. Then, within two months after Van Gogh left his monastic asylum, he was dead.

Beyond the entrance to Saint-Paul, one can take a walking tour of locations at which Van Gogh painted eight of his well-known works. At each site is a reproduction of the painting, for comparison with the actual view. The first is *The Mountains at Saint-Rémy*. In the foreground of the painting is a small house; in the background, the peaks of the Alpilles Mountains. The tour exists because, of course, it is fascinating to view the great paintings alongside, so to speak—in the very space and prospect—what gave rise to them. This is the world (as I am seeing it), and this is how Van Gogh saw it. How alike. How different. How totally the product of imagination, of hope, desire, fear, foreboding. How to tell the difference among them all?

What is also fascinating, in an entirely different way, beyond matters of aesthetics and creation—yet somehow the same?—is that the area in *The Mountains at Saint-Rémy*, just behind the house, is where Glanum stands, perhaps fifty yards from where Van Gogh painted, though Van Gogh would not have known this, since the ruins of Glanum were not uncovered until thirty-one years after his death: the world's, and history's, pentimento, marking off the invisible boundaries of all we can and cannot see—can ever understand completely in all our certainty.

Saint-Paul has cared for the mentally ill for much of its thousand-year history. It still does. Quiet and reverent in its atmosphere, as one would expect, the monastery guards the privacy of its current residents while earning funds through its Van Gogh connection. For a fee, one can enter and visit a replica of the small, sparsely furnished room in which Van Gogh lived. A brief video movingly considers both the man's artistic genius and the human dimensions of his illness. A note from the current director of the institutional program astutely even asks that travelers not reduce their visit to mere tourism, in disregard of the human being who suffered. The visitor cannot help but ponder the nature of that suffering—the daily struggle of a human life—against the product history makes of it.

By the time I left the monastery grounds, hours of roaming and solitary consideration had led me deep into myself. The ancient and recent impulses to conflict, the sources of inner turmoil, the search for accommodation to circumstance and peace, pressed against me like a humid skin. From the front gate of Saint-Paul, I walked the long avenue of trees to which Van Gogh, in his illness, was often accompanied by an attendant to paint. And in the curve of the road before me, in the onion-domed tree hoods bending concavely as if under some unseen pressure of sky, in the curling profile of the Alpilles' slopes cutting geometries out of the air, I suddenly saw, in utter revelation, *in the world*, the startling, swirling visions that seemed, before then, always surely the product of Van Gogh's eyes alone.

Universal Art Gallery (Opening soon)

They hang themselves
long before some canvas gets stretched
between any two imaginations.
And the photographs
reproduce on their own, develop in place
ahead of a shuttering eye:
such images as no artist makes
but renders service to.

They claim all the cornered walls
of the large and airy space,
take title of every geometry,
frame themselves
as round and rolling hips like hills
horizontal in the grass,
or envision beyond plain sight
the colors of a form
there is no shape to mold.
They insert themselves in flip-bin copies
of an Adirondack lake
or replicate unnumbered
those anointed moments that might be us
in whoever's kissed or fallen figure
on one of those days we all remember.

They develop on a film
of organ tissue and self:
brain's brief charge against
the emulsion of experience.
The patrons cannot buy
these ephemera they capture
like themselves in the mirror;
they own them all in common.
In a continuum of sight
along a corridor of blank and wondrous faces,
gargoyles grimace, soup cans jingle,
and innocents flee themselves.
It's all a fire in the recess
of a spot in the back,
down the stairs at the end
of a far, narrow hallway.

We stand there at angles,
our eyes like white diamonds,
and stare beneath a lifetime's
long and lurid, neon flicker.

Minnie

(Excerpt from *The Twentieth Century Passes*,
a memoir of my father's life)

By the time I was born, three of my grandparents were already dead. They had died young, in their early 60s, just before and after the birth of my sister ten years before me. My parents had had me, their third child, late for those days, my father at 42. The only grandparent my brother and I knew was Minnie, who had left Dad in infancy, as had her husband, Yoina, to travel to a new life in America. During my first decade, Minnie had already entered her 70s, but she looked, to a child, a hundred, and with her square, weathered face, the stocky block of her body, and her kerchiefed head, she could have been, during her frequent Sunday visits to our Queens Village garden apartment, any Babushka plucked the day before from a field in Podolia. And by then, she had been living in the United States for nearly fifty years.

We felt no love for Minnie. We had, the three of us, very early on some idea of what she had not been to our father, and it would have been otherwise, anyway, not easily accomplished, without some assistance, to turn from Howdy Doody and Captain Kangaroo to the peasantry under Czar Nicholas II. Minnie would arrive dutifully retrieved by my father, Mac, from her apartment off the Grand Concourse in the Bronx, to which he would return her, by car, at the end of the afternoon—two round trips of two-to-three hours each for every Sunday visit. Minnie would visit us along with her companion, Charlie, a large, round, gruff old American character with neatly parted and lacquered black hair and a fat cigar permanently chewed into the corner of his mouth. Imagine him beside Damon Runyon at a Jack Dempsey fight. Like everything else about the history of our family prior to our birth cries, we never got it entirely straight or clear from Mom, but apparently Charlie, who was some fair number of years younger than Minnie, was actually her first or second cousin, and her seduction of him away from a promising career (One must do uncounted mental crunches and endless stretching to imagine Minnie as seducer.) was a scandal in its day. Charlie was always friendly in his crusty way, but—he had, after all, shacked up with Minnie—also a being too foreign to contemplate for the suburban-ized children of Eisenhower's America.

Minnie was odd and distant and vastly inappropriate. On every visit, we would be brought before her at the dining room table as if in presentation to an idiot Queen, all terse and awkward decorum, in anticipation, as it were, of a detached and senseless laugh. Minnie would beam a smile of grandmotherly pleasure upon us and fix somewhere on each face one of those gross, heavily smeared lipstick kisses of comic, Woody Allen reminiscence. There was no other effort at contact with us. What there was, until Minnie grew too old and the visits ceased, was the ritual of found-gift giving. Planted at the table, each grandchild in turn beside her, Minnie would reach into and draw out from large Alexander's or Mays department store shopping bags a succession of soiled and broken toys that she had retrieved from the street: punctured rubber balls, wheel-less cars, half-used pencils, lone figurines, all held up with wonder before our eyes as if baubles brought from China. Sharyn, Jeffrey, and I would receive each gift in a manner of stupefied thanks, and then pass it to one parent, who would pass it to the other, who would next, for safekeeping, place the item into a bag, which would later, after Minnie's departure, complete the cycle of its existence as a garbage bag finally to be disposed of. Gift giving over, we grandchildren would depart—to leave the adults to their adult time together—but not before being quietly directed to go to the bathroom to wash our hands.

Sometime after Minnie divorced Yoina—sometime before the Russian Revolution—she returned to the United States and remarried. This marriage produced one of my father's four American-born half siblings, a brother, Jack. What became of Minnie's second husband before the Galsworthian scandal with Charlie, I do not know. Yoina was more productive in his second marriage, springing off my father's two other half brothers and half sister. These uncles and aunts made of Yoina, along with, of course, Aunt Goldie, were the foreign or strange, always affectively estranged, extended family that served to set for my siblings and me the bounds of family love very narrowly nuclear.

Around the time of my brother Jeff's Bar Mitzvah, Mac and Helen had a falling out with Minnie's American-born son, Jack, and his second wife. It was useless to try to find out precisely why. From the little I know, it was no one's finest hour, neither Jack's nor my parents', and as such, not characteristic of my parents' behavior. I gathered from my mother that there had been, over time, some growing jealousies and tensions leading up to the Bar Mitzvah, even, on my mother's part, some unverifiable suspicion of a secret, ugly act by Jack's wife against our family, against, in fact, me—a phony call to my mother at work that I had been rushed from school to the hospital with a ruptured spleen— the outcome was that Jack and his wife were not invited to the celebration. Not surprisingly this ruptured the relationship, and the two families (and Goldie, too, of course, whose bond to Mac was grafted onto bone) did not talk for over ten years, until Minnie's death in 1972.

Long before her death, Minnie's health had become too fragile to sustain any longer those occasional trips to our apartment, so my father assumed sole responsibility for maintaining contact with her. The rest of us, including Mom, fell out of Minnie's life without regret. Almost every Sunday, even after our move to the much-longer-distance-away Rockaway, Mac would drive to the Bronx to spend an hour or so visiting with his mother and then return. He did this early enough that I, a lazy and soporific teen, had barely begun my day by the time he returned. I was not too sleepy, though, to observe Mac's appearance when he came home. I would spy him, elbow on the kitchen table, his grave face sunk into his hand, hear him say to my mother how it drained all his spirit to see the way Minnie lived, and how she behaved toward him. Minnie's apartment was just off the Grand Concourse, which through the first half of the twentieth century had been the destination of upwardly mobile, Jewish poor relocating from the Lower East Side of Manhattan. By the 1970s, it was long since run down and its own form of Lower East Side to new generations of Spanish-speaking immigrants. Minne's apartment, my father said—what Minnie permitted him to see of it—was filthy and in disrepair. She would not let Dad past the kitchen—only just beyond the apartment's entrance, so that is where they sat, at the table, and had their visits. It was where Minnie kept at her side the shopping bag in which, Mac presumed, were the bank books and the cash Minnie had hoarded over an ungenerous lifetime of unskilled labor and which she wouldn't let from her side or sight even with her son. If Minnie needed to leave the room, she took the bag with her. If Mac tried to ease her mind, she would berate him.

When Minnie finally died, in her mid 80s, I think it was a relief to Mac. She broke her hip from a fall in the kitchen, where she lay on the floor undiscovered for days and died. The building superintendent smelled her decomposing body, called Jack, who called my father for the first time in eleven years, and my grandmother's death fulfilled a crucial pattern of her life in drawing her children together as a consequence of her having left them.

At the time Minnie died, Sharyn had just moved to Denver, hometown of her second husband, and Jeff was on the hippie tour of Europe, so it fell to Mac and me, at nineteen, along with Jack and his youngest son, to sort through Minnie's belongings and to clean out her apartment. The sad reminder of our reunion at Minnie's apartment, in an old Jewish neighborhood, was just how much the four of us were alike, my immigrant father and his American brother, my American cousin and American me. The pleasure of that reminder mixed with the sordidness of the task. The remainder of Minnie's apartment was all my father had guessed it to be. The living room, which he had not been allowed to view, we discovered to be stacked from floor to the ceiling with boxes. There were a couple of corridors through them, one leading to Minnie's bedroom, and the other to a cot at the far corner of the living room, to which Charlie had been banished, cast from Minnie's bed at some undetermined loss of her pleasure. Charlie had died a year or so before. He had lain in his cot, gangrene spreading along his legs, until, finally, Jack had discovered his condition and had him removed to a hospital, where the legs were amputated, and Charlie soon died.

Opening the boxes was a treasure hunt of bizarre and perplexing discoveries. Many were filled with old magazines. Many held objects wrapped in thirty-year-old newspapers: a plate, a candy dish, an old plastic baby doll. There were cockroaches everywhere.

The plain truth is that there was nothing Minnie had that anyone would have wanted, and Jack soon enough arranged through the super to have the apartment's belongings junked. We were searching for money. Bank books and cash. In addition to those Mac correctly supposed to be in Minnie's shopping bag, he and Jack both anticipated more to be in the bedroom, and they were right. But it took most of a day of sifting through dirty linens and clothes to find them all. We found one hidden among the pages of a book in the very bottom drawer of a tall dresser. Mac, in search of more, sat on the queen-sized bed to peer into one of the night tables, and in an instant jumped to his feet as a score of roaches charged from beneath the mattress and raced pell-mell across the bed cover.

We held handkerchiefs to our mouths. We wiped away the perspiration. We all bore into the task, but we observed and exclaimed for the others to hear just for the feeling of solidarity. Then Jack, who was searching the closet floor, called out.

"Look at this," he said, and he wheeled around.

There, before our eyes and our speechless selves, he held out a sandwich-sized plastic baggie in which were roiling perhaps a hundred roaches, one single, mass of black and brown bugs crawling and spilling over one another in an aimlessness and ugliness of human disgust. And each of us knew, amid our ordinary wonder at what the bag was doing in the closet, and how the roaches had come to be in it, and what they were all doing in it together, that that bag was it. That bag was everything. It was all, and we would never forget it.

At the end of the day, sick with fatigue and too much life, we entered off the other side of the Grand Concourse what was even then the relic of an older time—a New York cafeteria. For decades, when it thrived, Jewish immigrants had sat at its crowded tables, in the memory of pogroms and hard journeys, and argued with one another and made each other laugh.

"Listen, Shlomo, could've been worse—could've been me!"

The four of us sat amid their echoes and salved ourselves with food and drink, each of us weary in his private wonder—chewing, swallowing— at the squalor of the spirit that produces such putrefaction of the flesh.

Then we parted, to speak again, and drove our separate ways, my father and I back over the Tri-Borough Bridge, lofting us high over the East River, the Bronx, Manhattan, and Queens, our destination. Mac drove us home, his eyes fixed before him—as they had been since the dirt and rutted ways of peasant Ukraine—on the road ahead. I was already looking backward.

The Twentieth Century Passes

(For my mother and father)

1.

There is no way to know where she lost it
—along the way, or where the concrete
steps reminded her that nothing belongs to us anyway,
not even ourselves. Her father owned a kiosk
on Second Avenue and Eighth Street,
green and shuttered at night
like the sleeping world,
all its wondrous and awful news now
old and locked away.
He sold many Jewish papers: *The Daily Forward*,
which they moved, unlatching the gated
years, latching them
behind. She has told me this
many times, but for the first time (always, for her)
only since the earth rose up
to meet her from the drive of Lawry's restaurant.
She can still smell
at the threshold of the doorway
under the stoop on Fourth Street
the odor of an unfavored child (who married when she could)
though she cannot place it anymore.
We eat our sandwiches.
"Did you like tuna?" she asks, as if puzzling the mysteries.
I nod: "It was my favorite."
At that, we both turn to Katharine Hepburn, sixty years ago
and taut as a bowstring, wonder if the stars remember
every escapade and kiss, or if sometimes in the darkness,
they sit and only stare
at some actor on the screen.

2.

The way his hand trembles a little
reaching with the key to unlock
the lock that opens
to his home again. How he cannot hear
the lips he cannot see
beside him. How in the spreading fog
through which he reaches, he might see
a dirt road and a wagon passing
a short, theological
bearded and mercantile man
crossing in the wagon's traffic:
then fierce riders on bridled fury
madly grinning at the bit, their cry and whinny
and his grandfather bleeding and bootless on the ground ...

The key finds its home
in a century of terror—
these are its chambers,
its tumblers made to fit by some smith
of hidden craft.
There is simple business now:
a kettle to fill, the tea to brew,
a piece of fish, some bread,
a stretch of the long, unyielding muscle that has tread
the mill from Orinin to Warsaw, Nairobi to Palestine,
to gyms throughout New York and Woodland Hills.
Some curls and presses, too.
What weights are those to carry?
On the balcony, beside his dozing wife, in forgetfulness
he wills to happen, he sits and fills the distance without care.
Though he cannot see it, he knows
it is out there, and the salt-sea Pacific
breathes clean in his nose.
This is the key; these
are the chambers
that tumbled in dreams in the night.
From hard beginnings sometimes
easy ends.

Talking with My Father, 93, while Reading the Sunday Paper over Breakfast, Distinguishing the First from the Second Time

(Excerpt from *The Twentieth Century Passes*)

It was like a naming of parts, parts of a life, parts never named, named but then renamed, names of events, unknown, to be reknown, reordered, remembered. Membered. Parts. Of a life.

"I've been there," Mac said.

"Where?"

"Where—

(The repetition as an impatience, a matter-of-factness, an "I lived it; why would it need to have been told? It was.")

—Nairobi."

"Nairobi. Kenya. You've been to Nairobi, Kenya. When the hell were you ever in Nairobi, Kenya?"

"When. On the way here."

"What were you doing in Nairobi?"

"They took us there."

"They. *(I am his son.)* Who's they? They took you there from where?"

"How do I know? A Jewish organization."

"From where?"

"Where would they take me from?—From Russia."

"Russia? But you'd already left Russia. You were in Poland."

"I came *back*."

"You came back from Poland to Russia? You never told us that."

"Of course." (*Of course.*)

"Where'd you go from there?"

"From Russia?"

"From Nairobi."

"To London."

"London. Now he's been to London. By ship?"

"What then, by horse?"

"Where'd you go from there?"

"Then, I came here."

"I thought you came from Bremerhaven."

"That was the *second* time."

(A second time.)

ReMembered, Parts of a life. Reordered. Recalled. Reknown. Names of events never named, renamed. Like a naming of parts. It was. It was told.

This New England Spring

I remember you:
unseasonably sad,
a wispy stalk, some straw
(your hair that color)
the wind might whirl away, wishing
probably, some man would—
make it all better, make you

                     not like straw.

And in the residual traces
of a plainly animal life
mere bone of memory,
steam of long, damp loam—
in recalling you—
do I recollect me, too?
You would join us
sometimes, Janet, David, and me,
in the glow of City College life
in those days when Nixon made history real,
and we, on early study-room mornings
alone by windows, in a bolt of sunlight
with a cigarette
read Camus to make our burdens so.
New York was drama then,
as now, nova of secret and public dreams
scorching young and old in its halo.
We gathered to argue in Philosophy Hall,
Ernesto back from Chile, Allende dead,
and all through the room, our lives in danger
of uselessness.
We'd have taken the bus down
Convent Avenue, to the little Cuban place
David had discovered on 113th Street
and Broadway, sat at a foursquare table
in the back over suckling pig and Spanish wine,
an unexpected feast in the broadness of late afternoon,
and talked of elusive love, our brittle hearts, the world
we disbelieved. I remember you sitting, not talking
much, pleased, I think, to be part of it, to be

invited to this conclave of embryos
negotiating to become people.
I suspect you thought we were interesting;
so slender were you and so scared
to dash yourself against the walls
and crash to the floor another awful time
as volubly as we did.
I don't even know where you came from.
So, what should I recover
from your namelessness to me,
save your likeness to some adjacent agony
you were too deep in yours to know?
And what is that in my life now?
Janet knew you—a girl like a strand of hair
so long, so limp,
with each small nib and knob of your face
in awkward relation to another—
your strangely fleeting smile
too timid to take its space in the air.
I found you oddly, shyly pretty,
but I was always feeling something
for the funny ones
who were really only my bent light
refracted through another.
So, what are you, then, to me? And whom should I remember?
That moment—the four of us—was very brief
and the three of us, you know—without you—
were not so very much.
I haven't seen David in twenty years,
but I'm sure it was Janet, not long after,
who called me in Virginia
and described how you'd traveled to Israel
to work on a kibbutz—
"Oh, *that* self-discovery," I reflexively mocked—
and how a few good friends you'd actually made
had come to your room to take you to dinner
and opened the door to your naked body hanging
limp from a beam, your neck wound round
with the clothes you'd worn that day in the field.
The field I imagine as the color of straw—
some straw the wind carries away.
I confess to you, here on the page
now, as I write this:
I've thought of you too little
to claim you
as you make this claim on me

that I've lived these twenty-five or -six years since
and thought of you—
how the wide world's deep, devouring hole
had opened up, to your despair, in you
and your silent terror at its bottomless pull.
I've thought how I sat by myself once
in the corner seat of a crowded car
(the faces hanging over me)
of the subway at my stop
and saw no reason, ever, to rise—
and how I held on. That's what
they say, you know: "Hold on."
I think of what we didn't know
that day you dissolved in the field,
the world wind blowing through you
like the disappearing dream
of your unknown self:
that we live there—we were too young
to know—and it comes, effort by effort
in a daily way, out of our wintered souls
like the slow surprise of spring—
this New England spring
I could never have guessed I'd have
so long and far from who we were—
so close to whom I grew to be.
So, what should I remember then?
And who are you to me?
It comes in the rains and mists
that drift over the fir and pine tops,
comes in the river's rush around
a water-parting boulder—
my bicycle's wheeling bloom along
the rise and fall of roads.
My keyboard's tap, the coffee's steam,
the wide lay of the light on earth
as if a lucent skin surrounds us—
it's only a month before I go,
but there's someone waiting
it took so long to find.
It's not the everlasting spring we dreamed of—
everlasting doesn't last—
but you can make each moment
and a month of days—oh, I can't tell you;
you have to know yourself. It's just that
New England made me think of you—
this New England, now—

and I wished that you could see
how fine it is, the brink of time
from which you leaped
that's become so broad for me:
you're standing on it, glancing up
as I pass, glancing back at you;
this one unbounded moment bubbles
up from our bounded lives;
a faintly mirrored film
trembles in the current that surrounds us.
There, where all we hope we might be born for,
every choice we've yet to make
in every instant that awaits us,
plays across the insubstantial screen,
the eventual detail rises
an August moon.
And I remember you in me.

Pine Tree Lodge
On Route 66 — West Side
GALLUP, NEW MEXICO

The American Road

Route 66 begins in the imagination. That there is a better place. That it lies in the westward distance. That every rock and tree 'round every road that bends delivers an undiscovered world. That lives, drawn to where the sun sets on what those who live them never before have seen, can begin again. That the road is the way.

Route 66 also begins where Adams Street starts, just blocks from Lake Michigan, sprouting westward from the avenue also called Michigan, in Chicago. It continues for 2,448 miles south and west through eight states of the Union and countless states of anticipation to the Santa Monica Pier on the Pacific Ocean. It was at its inception, and remains today, the final step in the American mythic journey of individual self-realization.

When the route was inaugurated on November 11, 1926, the era of the automobile was little more than 25 years old. The first Federal-Aid Road Act had been passed just ten years earlier, and the Bureau of Public Roads had been authorized by the Federal Highway Act of 1921 to aid in the development of a paved, two-lane interstate highway system. Route 66 underwent several improvements and realignments during the 1930s and into the 50s, but when President Roosevelt authorized a "National System of Interstate Highways" in 1944, finally funded by President Eisenhower's Federal-Aid Highway Act of 1956, the rise of the current interstate highway system and the decline of Route 66 were already set in motion. Only 18 years separated the beginning of Route 66 and what would ultimately lead to its end as an officially commissioned and active U.S. Highway.

It was Cyrus Avery, of the American Association of State Highway and Transportation Officials, who became known as the "Father of Route 66." Avery led the effort to persuade the federal government of the need, and was ultimately charged by Secretary of Agriculture Howard M. Gore with establishing the first U.S. highway from the Eastern United States to the West Coast, by creating a network of existing roads and filling in the blanks.

As with any public project, nothing was simple or easy, and there were battles to be fought over the starting point, the states to be traversed, and even the highway's number designation. The road was not even fully paved until 1937. But at Route 66's inception, for the first time, it was possible for a lone individual—never mind families and larger groups—to set off, without being a mountain man, or signing on with a wagon train, or giving oneself up to the timetables and direction of a railroad, on a journey to the west.

Yet, Route 66 was directly in the line of descent from those earlier pathways westward. Only five years after Lewis and Clark reached the Pacific in 1805, the first commercial expedition into the Western wilderness was made by John Jacob Astor's "Astorians." The mountain men and fur trappers who followed the earliest expeditions into the Rockies flourished until about 1840, by which time the supply of beaver had diminished and the last great, annual trapper "rendezvous" took place. Popular lore has portrayed the mountain man as a loner finding his own way in the unmapped wild, and there were such men. Most, however, were trappers commercially employed and working in groups of forty to sixty that broke up into teams of two or three. This tension, between the myth of a single person seeking the realization of his individual will and of a larger collective pursuing a commercial or social aim, arises everywhere in the migration westward.

When the beaver were depleted, and there was too little left to trap, many of the mountain men who wished to continue to live outside of civilization hired on as guides for the new wagon trains leaving from Missouri for unsettled land. The trappers had found the way, and now, from St. Louis, St. Joseph, and Independence, not only individuals seeking fortune at gold strikes and elsewhere, but whole families seeking new lives were heading west. In the heyday of the Western wagon train, from 1840 to 1860, as many as 500,000 people migrated along the Oregon, California, and Santa Fe trails.

These trails became permanent routes west, but as coordinates on maps and rutted wagon-wheel trails, they were paths for the most intrepid—of which the United States has never had shortage—but not for the ordinary lone individual or family. Phenomena like the Pony Express, and the telegraph that spelled the short-lived Express' demise, provided the first sense of coast-to-coast communication, but they were not a means of travel.

Only with the driving of that last, golden spike connecting the Union Pacific and the Central Pacific Railroads in 1869, had a means of transportation been established that enabled the free flow of people, without the daunting hardship and risk of wilderness travel, between the nation's Eastern origins and its Western expansion. It had taken just short of 64 years from the date Lewis and Clark reached their destination across an uncharted wilderness until the completion of the first, fixed, permanent, regular, and safe means of transportation across it. Where once an overland journey would have taken months—it had taken Lewis and Clark twenty—or a journey by ship around Cape Horn weeks, on June 4, 1876, the Transcontinental Express traveled from New York City to San Francisco in 83 hours and 39 minutes.

Before and after the railroad, there was also the stagecoach, for some decades a regular fixture of western commerce and travel. But companies such as the Butterfield Overland Express Company were primarily government- and private-mail haulers and, like Wells Fargo, movers of bank funds. For the nine people crammed into a semi-weekly Celerity coach for the typical twenty-five day, bone-jarring, cold and snowy, or hot, sweaty, and smelly journey from Missouri to California, the fare was around $200, or about $4,000 in today's money, more or less the price of a one-way ticket on the Concorde SST over its lifespan. If you could afford it, you took the stagecoach before the transcontinental line was completed, or because it went places the railroad didn't, not to celebrate your individual freedom as an American to travel where you wished.

The railroad, on the other hand, moved thousands, hundreds of thousands—millions. Along with the Homestead Act of 1862, it completed the settlement of the West.

The Homestead Act offered free title to 160 acres—after five years, if you worked the land and improved it. In contrast, the railroads sold the land along their right-of-way, the land they had been granted by the federal government as an incentive to undertake the transcontinental enterprise. The completion of the Transcontinental Railroad lives on in the popular historical imagination as one of the great moments in the building of the American nation, and it is certainly that. An extraordinary technical feat and a permanent conquest of nature cannot be denied. But here again, as with every inroad to the West, that tension between the individual and the collective is visible.

An individual picks up from New York, or Philadelphia, or the Ohio River Valley, or even somewhere in Europe, and alone or with his family makes his way finally, by train, to Nebraska, Wyoming, California, or another state, to start afresh. The railroad is available for travel, however, because the government had its grander social and commercial goals, granted land—and its natural resources—to the enterprises commissioned to lay the track, and even subsidized the construction.

The railroad is there to be used because legislators succumbed to wholesale bribery from lobbyists in the form of cash and corporate bonds. It is there because the owners and operators of the Union Pacific Railroad established the shell company, Credit Mobilier—the Enron of its day, owned by the same majority shareholders as the Union Pacific—to which to award the construction contract and bill back the railroad, subsidized by the federal government (and risk-taking private investors), multiple times the actual cost of materials and labor.

Once the Transcontinental Railroad was established, the railroads also went into the business of luring settlers to migrate to the West. They offered reasonable prices for the land, good credit terms to enable purchase, showings of parcels, and even established European offices with representatives to attract additional emigration across the Atlantic. The settlers would populate the land the railroads traversed and help establish the railroad towns that would both service and feed off the railroad. Thus is the goal of a westward expansion fulfilled. Thus does the American mythos of individual initiative and self-determination run up against a contradiction. And that is how it remained for almost 60 more years.

But if our world is anything, it is a world of contradiction. However settlers may have arrived—by someone else's wagon train, stage coach, or train, or by steamer from another part of the world—whatever corporate hucksterism or nationalistic boosterism had sold them an idea about the circumstances toward which they traveled that was not entirely in accordance with reality (disgruntled natives not entirely glad you're coming, anyone?), they had made their own choices, determined their own wills, and endured hardships their neighbors would not undertake. They possessed the independence and strength to travel far from unhappy or unsatisfactory conditions that others less daringly abided, and they felt no less individual because they aimed to shape their destinies within a web of relation and influence they could not always see around them.

Perhaps that is why the lone cowboy on his horse, crossing the panhandle, passing among the mesas, a speck on a vast prairie beneath an enormous sky—what so few, in fact, ever were—became our resonant American myth. Nothing is ever how we portray it, but our symbols are what we feel, and we feel for a reason. The cowboy, as we see him, is singular and integrally himself within the natural world. His kindnesses are not mandated, but his own. His cooperation is given, not required. And if he's of a mind, whenever he's of a mind, he'll go his own way. Just point his horse's head like a compass, and move on.

Yet, how many could really live that dream?

Beginning November 11, 1926, anyone.

And with the affordability of Ford's Model T—soon to be a fixture on the new Highway 66—the automobile was quickly developing into what it would not take very long to become, the singular and democratic mode of transportation of the 20th century and beyond. Route 66, the first transcontinental interstate highway, was created to serve it.

It is true that in the years before the opening of the route, there had developed the romance of train travel, and the train has its romancers still. Stand in so many small towns across America—a town, say, like Dwight, Illinois, through which Route 66 runs—and watch the train pass through, even now. Listen to its whistle. Hear it "moan mournfully," as Thomas Wolfe's Eugene Gant heard it. Far places, it says. Distant lives. The great, wide world. Teasing you with its call. Passing on. For so many who longed for experience, the train's receding rumble, the lingering whisper of it gone, uttered the great paradox of the nation—that while one might live, it seemed, smack-dab in the middle of it all, one felt stranded so far from everything that was happening. To live in the middle, it turned out, was to reside at the edges. To move to the center meant to travel to the boundaries, because the boundary—the frontier—is where the "other" is, and the other is experience.

Before Route 66, in any of America's countless small towns, with the train seeming to emphasize more the distance of it all than the nearness, it must have been hard, at times, really to comprehend it as one nation. Of the nearly 3 million miles of highway in America in 1920, only 36,000 had the all-weather surface to sustain automobile traffic. Today's interstates are massive arteries. The roads before 66 were capillaries, so small and spindly before the size of the country and the scope of its ambition, who could have truly imagined, standing in one of those towns and looking out, the extent and oneness of that to which, in fact, those roads did not adequately connect them?

After Route 66, though, small towns were never quite so much that again, because the highway not only takes you to the other; it brings the other to you. People passing through, people you would otherwise never have met, needing places to stay, to eat, to fill up on gas—even recreation, in odd, roadside attractions: petting zoos, trading posts, statuary, motel rooms in teepees. Spend a dollar. Make a dollar.

The first of Route 66's four distinct eras began with only 800 of its 2,448 miles paved. The remainder was graded dirt, gravel, asphalt-covered brick, or even planks of wood. But those early travelers came.

Starting as far east as Chicago, they would drive through Illinois, Missouri, Kansas, Oklahoma, Texas, New Mexico, Arizona, and California. They traveled through the Ozarks, the Oklahoma prairie, the Texas Panhandle, the Great Plains, the Mountains of Northern Arizona, the Arizona and California deserts. They had to prepare for cold and great heat. On long stretches of road, a Model T might be far from civilization in the midst of forbidding geography. Still, it was an adventure, with picnics beside the car, for those picking up and moving, and for those inaugurating the tradition of the long-distance road trip.

From the beginning, Route 66 was promoted across the nation. The National U.S. 66 Highway Association dubbed the route "The Main Street of America." A marathon foot race, The Bunion Derby, was organized to follow the route in 1928. The soon-to-be-famous sequential Burma Shave signs appeared along the route:

> *A peach*
> *looks good*
> *with lots of fuzz*
> *but man's no peach*
> *and never was*
> *Burma Shave.*

It didn't hurt either that in its last years, a Model T could be purchased for as little as $290, only $3,000 in today's money, or nearly three quarters the cost of that single 1860 stagecoach trip to California—for a car that was your own and would last.

It wasn't long before a new era dawned. The Depression put a crimp in road-trip tourism, but it, and the Dust Bowl, sent new legions, from Arkansas, Oklahoma, Kansas, and Texas, onto the road. It was the single greatest migration in American history. John Steinbeck, who drove what he and others then called Highway 66, to research his book, memorialized the route in *The Grapes of Wrath*, providing it with a new, and its most resonant, name:

> *... and they come into 66 from the tributary side roads,*
> *from the wagon tracks and the rutted country roads.*
> *66 is the mother road, the road of flight.*

Woody Guthrie sang:

> *Been on this road for a mighty long time,*
> *Ten million men like me,*
> *You drive us from your town, we ramble around,*
> *And got them 66 Highway Blues.*

In the end, one quarter of the Dust Bowl population uprooted itself and moved away. As many as 2.5 million people left the Great Plains, nearly 400,000 of them coming to California, and they did it along Route 66. As no road had been since the 19th century wagon trails, the mother road was at the center of the American story.

The route played a vital role again during its third era, that of the Second World War. During the nation's massive mobilization for the conflict, troop convoys and armor rumbled across the country on the highway. All around Route 66, in the Mojave Desert, at the Desert Training Center, California-Arizona Maneuver Area—the largest military training area in the history of warfare—General George Patton prepared the troops of what would become his Western Task Force for their coming North Africa campaign.

Yet, while the route served, a road not constructed for military use was also severely debilitated by it, which pointed to the road's necessary and ultimate demise. The vast interstate system that would eventually replace it was, in part, summoned by military need.

Before the end, though, Route 66 had still to enter its last and most iconic period, the era of the postwar boom. Every other boom of those years from 1945-1960—in the economy and population, in education, with nearly 6 million veterans entering college or other schools on the GI Bill—echoed down the highway. Americans were traveling in numbers never before approached. The mobile society had begun. People moved to take new jobs, sought different environments and more favorable climates. The population shift tended toward the Southwest, the direction of Route 66. And vacation travel by car also took root on the route: Disneyland opened in 1955, and Route 66 very nearly took you to it, and to the Grand Canyon.

Part of the movement along the highway in the postwar years was among GIs who had trained and been stationed in the West and decided they liked it. One of those GIs was songwriter/actor Bobby Troup, who moved with his wife, Cynthia, from Harrisburg, Pennsylvania, to Los Angeles in 1946, to begin his career. She suggested they write a song about the trip, and once they connected to the highway, whispered in Troup's ear, "Get your kicks on Route 66." He worked on the song for the rest of the trip, and Nat King Cole made it the hit that people old enough remember.

Other men Troup's age spent the 1950s taking their families on those auto vacations along the route. It is many of their children, and some surviving elders, who continue to revere Route 66 today, for trips to the Meramec Caverns in Missouri, where the Jesse James gang hid out, for the Painted Desert, for the architecture of roadside motels and diners, for the varied small town and regional cultures that were the American story the highway told.

In 1952, Highway 66 was dedicated the Will Rogers Highway, in memory of the humorist and performer born in Claremore, Oklahoma, yet one more stop along the Route 66 way. In 1952, you couldn't get more American than Will Rogers, and maybe still today: said Rogers once, when asked his political affiliation, "I'm not a member of any organized political party; I'm a Democrat!"

Most of all, though—a prerequisite for all the other loves—those who cherish Route 66 are lovers of the open road. If you think of Route 66, at some point you'll think of Jack Kerouac's novel, *On the Road*—even though the book never mentions the route, and its characters, Sal Paradise and Dean Moriarity, are often, clearly, not traveling on it. So it is for Tod and Buz, the main characters of the famed 1960-64 television show, *Route 66*. Watch one of the episodes from the recent, complete DVD reissue, and you'll as likely find Martin Milner and George Maharis in Mississippi as

Arizona. To love the road means to love Route 66; love Route 66, and you love the road, wherever it is. Open-road travel is a state of being, not a state of the Union, or even necessarily a state of exactitude, which is why it is arguable at what street in Chicago, really, or where truly in Los Angeles, Route 66 actually starts and ends. Which alignment you talkin' about? '26? '37? '52?

As it often is with legends, they capture the imagination even as their subjects are already passing from the scene. By the time of the television show, the new interstate system was well underway, and Route 66 was on the way out. Little by little, new interstates—55 in Illinois, 44 in Missouri, 40 for much of the way further, 10 into Los Angeles—replaced large sections of 66, large sections of which were old and worn and far from what modern automobile travel required. The last stretch of the highway was bypassed in Arizona in 1984, and in 1985, Route 66 was decommissioned as an official U.S. highway. You won't even find it on most road maps anymore, although you can often find it on Yahoo and Google Maps.

As it often is, again, with legends, the subjects are not long gone before the effort to memorialize and revive them begins. By the early 1990s, state and national Route 66 associations were forming, picture and guide books and memorial tomes began to appear—a magazine and many websites now exist. There are books that rate the restaurants and hotels along the way. Association members have adopted sections of road for care. While some towns died from the loss of the highway, others now seek to revive and sustain themselves by proudly promoting their Route 66 heritage.

Because sections of the road are forever gone, while others, overgrown with grass or simply abandoned, are roads to nowhere; because in some places the road was rerouted around towns, or the new interstates, as frontage road; and because various alignments offer different alternatives, such as the Santa Fe loop of the pre-1937 alignment, driving 66 today is as great an adventure as always, but not an easy task. Though the state-by-state revival has long stretches of the route carefully marked by new, "Historic" Route 66 signs, many large gaps will leave a traveler quite lost quite frequently. Some of the guidebooks offer turn-by-turn, even every-tenth-of-a-mile directions and signposts. This is an impressive feat over more than 2,400 miles, though the very first turn off of Adams Street in Chicago may be shown as 1.3 miles, while a couple of travelers will swear it is two. A crossing over an interstate may be indicated, counter-intuitively, as a right turn east when a check of another book after five miles will verify one's intuition and turn two travelers maddeningly around. Alternative guide-books will gain and lose your trust many times over the journey.

Particularly in Illinois and Missouri, old Route 66 is a patchwork of alignments cutting this way, switching that, through this little town, then that, marked, and then not marked. A navigator's nose must always be in a book, eyes rechecking directions, or the travelers are lost. Casual conversation and staying on course are a zero-sum game. Come Oklahoma (and beyond) and the traveling is easier, with Route 66 now the free road Oklahoma 66, a favored Oklahoman alternative to the interstate toll road.

There is sadness along the way, in what has so obviously been lost, in the ghost towns, in the poor towns, in the growing sameness of long, commercial, "business loop" strips with their chain stores and restaurants and fast food. Hunt a little, a couple of blocks one way or the other off the strip, and you'll discover the town's old main street, half the stores empty, the street deserted.

Still, as always, there are the profound pleasures and surprises of the road. You'll drive Cutter's Path, an original-alignment-and-cement, four-lane slice through a Missouri mountain that'll put you in your Model T eying bootleggers going the other way. You'll spend a night in Lebanon, Missouri, and learn that when the railroad came through, it wanted the town to give it land for free. The town refused. To make its point, the railroad laid its track a mile away. At which point, in turn, the town picked up and moved over to the track. So you could say in this case it was "show them," not "me."

You'll drive, suddenly and unexpectedly, through Commerce, Oklahoma, which, if you're a New Yorker of a certain age, is the birthplace of your boyhood idol, Mickey Mantle, and you'll feel fifteen again. Then, there is Weatherford, home of astronaut Thomas P. Stafford, and Claremore, where not only Will Rogers was born, but Lynn Riggs, author of *Green Grow the Lilacs*, from which the musical *Oklahoma* was adapted. Or as one town announced itself, the Burma Shave way, on the way in:

> *A small town*
> *With a big heart*
> *Where everybody*
> *Is somebody.*

In Clinton, Oklahoma, you may encounter 30+ French bikers in the Route 66 museum. Marc, the leader, will reminisce about watching the television show as a child and tell you oh, no, he never gets lost—he's got GPS. Ask the cashier if she often gets large groups like that, and she'll tell you she's got 48 Norwegian bikers due in that afternoon. It could be enough to make you wonder whether, if all Europeans really do think that all Americans are cowboys, maybe some of them actually don't mind it. They wouldn't mind driving to the dead end of an abandoned stretch of the route, just to imagine what was on the other side. They wouldn't mind the best breakfast of their journey at Debbie's Diner, near Canute, Oklahoma, or Debbie asking them to spread the word. (Spreading the word.)

There will be ghost towns like Glenrio, right on the Texas–New Mexico border, and hours on the road with no other car in sight, and the long, long swath cut from New Mexico ranch land of 1926 dirt and gravel alignment, far from the interstate, reminding you, as all open-road travel does, of your singular presence amid the enormity of the natural world. The old ranching couple mending fence will wave, knowing just who you are in your road car with out-of-state plates, and exactly what you are doing there.

There will be the mesa you round, and the moment you stop and get out of the car to feel the silence, hear the stillness, listen to no wind blow through you. A deer will fright on a low crag across the road, start and stop, bound to the cliff top and lift its ears, run as the earth rumble grows. From out of the pass, the train will come, long and steady, brown cars, red cars, yellow, reminding you, as you stand and watch, that while you are always alone, you are always connected.

And then, finally—*at last,* you may think—curving and cornering through the mountain switchbacks on the stretch between Kingman and Oatman, Arizona, the old gold mining and Western town where burros roam and Clark Gable and Carole Lombard spent their honeymoon night— you catch sight of the wide, sweeping valley below, and still more mountains beyond, and you wonder, as they must have back in '26, and on how many horses and wagons before: Does it never end? Does it go on forever, this country? Is there always another valley, another mountain, another plain? They say there is an ocean.

But you will arrive. And the road will return you to yourself, whether it is the route called 66 or another. Because Route 66, as Kerouac knew, as the makers of the TV series knew, is just the emblem of the open road, which is to say: its essence. We are alone and connected, and the road tells us both.

In a world in which the daily coffee Americans buy may or may not enable a Guatemalan farmer to live, or the sport shoes we wear lead a Chinese child to labor 12 hours a day in a sweatshop; in a world in which the toot we put up our nose loses a child's policeman-father his head in Rosarito, and the computer we buy starts a new life for a young woman in Bangalore (and the gasoline we put in our tanks fuels the terror against us) —in such a world of six billion people, to insist we can live by the libertarian ideals of an 18th-century agrarian society of just under four million may seem a stretch of the common in sense. *And yet ... And yet ...*

And yet, there are those who recoil to think they are born into an ant colony of genetically and socially contracted roles and regulations, that they evacuate the womb to be captured by government forms, numbers, and imprints before they are even really people. (Though the number that gets you cash from the Bank of America drive-in machine when you're running low in Tulsa comes in pretty handy.)

On the road, at least—if not soon in Britain, at least still here—you can regain your anonymity, disappear into the human grove of earth at this overpass or that T, or along the "let's see where that goes." You can leave behind for a while the Middle East, and Darfur, and Tamil Tigers, and the forgotten prisons of Myanmar—the my God, your God, whose God, no God—and try to remember something. Maybe you recall it in the Petrified Forest or great Meteor Crater of Arizona, maybe in deserts, maybe in a bar.

It's like Buz used to say over the credits each week, as he and Tod would first set out all over again in their Corvette: "Goodbye, Pittsburgh. Hello, world."

There may be troubles behind and uncertainty ahead. But there is possibility, too. And while your destination lies before you, for now there is the journey. Winds come up, and they cease. Islands of white cloud hang suspended in the blue. Fields go by. Towns go by. Rivers and bridges. Mountain. Valley. Mesa. Butte. In what seems a dream of life, and not life, which is to say life at last, and not a dream, the rhythm of the road, the quick of perception—both lull you and drive you on. You are individual and alive, and everything that passes catches the sun.

Place

traveling

It's a road, behind and before. I wander it like dust,
with wind for a will.

Arizona, now, ranges over mountain and pass,
desert brush and Geronimo's ghost, for once
a watchful youth

while Los Angeles is leaving, spinner and lure
for a hungry eye, hooked, but never caught.
They're soft winds over those ocean dreams. They blow,
they blow.

Soon Oklahoma, the South, Virginia,
Michigan, the Northern Plains: the sweep and particular
of country and tale—also a vision. Deep breath and sigh, wide-eyed
I have seen this meadow, that rock, timber of a home long ago
I had always imagined.

Budapest, too, and Buenos Aires, and Asian jungle
whose river snakes to a mountain source, the hidden life
from early springs. Sought a seed, too, where my father
sprang from Galicia, a cold and foreign soil in which to germinate
a Jew. How far, then, back to ramble home? Be gusted over Sinai sands?
Gather in the Great Rift Valley?

Where I come from, every feeling calls a name, every
name a habitation, a place of birth, and all my destinations merge
into me. When the Dutch first spied Manhattan's breast, and paid
with all the rich corruptions of the heart for every generation crossing
Brooklyn ferry, they opened up a harbor, carried human cargo
the city still unloads. Hudson wandered, too, up Mahicanittuk River
and never arrived beyond it.

Bordello Rooms

The way I do it is I stand in the middle. I've done it all over the world. I stand in the midst of a historic environ, and I conjure. I go to museums. I eat in the restaurants. I sit in the squares and inhale, with the lift of a hand to my nose, the daily life. I seek the raw or gentle splendor of nature. But my true destination, in all my travels, is the past. I seek the literary Paris of the Twenties in Old-World cobblestones, or that of the Revolution layers deeper. In Saint-Rémy-de-Provence, it is the path of Van Gogh's painting I follow, and again, though they were hidden from him, the ruins of ancient Glanum many levels below. I imagine, thirty years on, the youthful death fortune withheld from me in the Mekong Delta. I follow the flight of Depression migrants along Route 66. And I make pilgrimage, after his death, to the Ukrainian *shtetl* of my father's birth, near the Medieval city of Kamenets-Podolsk.

There is even a photo by Julia (my significant other, or SO, we call her; I'm her SOB) entitled, "Capturing Jay's Imagination."

It was our first night in Vienna, and we were walking without guidance, when we stumbled upon the Hofburg Palace, on the entrance, in fact, to what had been the private apartments of the royal family. Immediately, my imagination set to work, figuring before my eyes the horse-drawn carriages that once would have swept into the outdoor entrance rotunda to deposit their royal *Ärsche* home. No sooner had I voiced this imagining to Julia, but I was forced back by those nearly selfsame carriages (though Julia stood ground with her camera) delivering more modern derrieres to what turned out to be a charity event.

If only for an instant, in ignorance of the details, I had made it so. I had paddled back against the current of loss.

This time, I'm in the Arizona desert, gazing at the landscape as the dogs chase rabbits and roadrunners around me. My back is turned to Highway 80, to RVs and the other signs of post-19th-century life, though they are not plentiful. Before me, almost all around me, is an empty, sweeping, sometimes rolling expanse, ringed by a moonscape of mountains. It startles me with its beauty. I hadn't expected it. I'm only a mile from Tombstone.

And I conjure. It is easy enough to see—Doc Holliday or the Clantons, ghost-like, riding their horses through the brush, over the shallow gullies. Like a slow superimposition in a film, I can draw out of the atmosphere Wyatt Earp and Josie Marcus—the Jewish prostitute who was his third and final wife, of over forty years—talking by a bush as he woos her away from Sheriff Johnny Behan. What I imagine once more, probably more miraculously than anything else, is the notion that these people and the moments of their lives—because they have become so legendary—continue to occupy some alternate dimension of the coordinates that surround me. As if every period of time—every instant—persists in some fractional off-frame, a parallel universe just a little invisibly, dimensionally beyond sensory apprehension. Until I conjure. And then, I envisage that Earp and Marcus, in clandestine conversation in the desert in 1881, are an event somehow more concrete than my own occupation of that space, standing there in all my mundaneness in the desert of today, an experience the ephemeralness of which I exhale with every breath.

The famous line from John Ford's *The Man Who Shot Liberty Valance* is: "When the legend becomes fact, print the legend." But though there are disputes about many of the "facts" of Earp's life, there is little, really, about the genuinely legendary nature of the life. Testimonies to his fearlessness and strength of character, by men nearly his equal in legend, like Bat Masterson, are many. That, of the seven men who stood their ground during the gunfight at the O.K. Corral (really two lots down the street, but legends are created of words, and "two lots down from" doesn't work), three died, three were wounded, and only Earp emerged unscathed is firmly established. And we must concede the force and will of the man who led what is known as the three-week "Earp Vendetta Ride," in pursuit of the men who murdered his brother, Morgan, five months after the O.K. Corral, leaving anywhere from five to fifteen men dead.

The town lives up to its legend, too. It was named by the silver miner, Ed Schieffelin, who was told by soldiers at the nearby fort that the only stone he'd find in Apache country was his tombstone. It had—still has—the most compellingly named newspaper in journalism: *The Tombstone Epitaph*. ("Every tombstone needs one," said its founder, John Clum.) Of those buried on Boot Hill, by far the largest number were shot, or murdered in some other way. Many are of unknown identity. More than a few were killed by Apaches, as Tombstone is in Apache country, in what is now known as Cochise County. Some were hanged or lynched. Of one, it says on his grave marker:

Here Lies
George Johnson
Hanged By
Mistake
1882
He Was Right
We
Was Wrong
But We Strung

Him Up
And Now He's
Gone.

By my rough count, in just the years 1881-1882 (The gunfight at the O.K. Corral took place on October 26, 1881; Morgan Earp was murdered March 18, 1882.), about 40 people were killed in a town of roughly 5,000, nearly one every two weeks. It was a helluva town in which to try to live and not unlikely die.

Wyatt Earp was one of the few of his stature to die of old age, at 80 in Los Angeles in 1929. Silent-film cowboy, Tom Mix, wept at Earp's grave. Doc Holliday died of tuberculosis at 36. Big Nose Kate, Doc Holliday's lover, lived to five days shy of 90. Hungarian by birth, she was the daughter of the physician to the Emperor Maximilian of Mexico, who was deposed three years after her family's arrival. A long, sordid journey and tale took her from that life to Tombstone. When she died in 1940, it was in the Arizona Pioneers Home, which was founded to offer a refuge to the aging pioneers of the Arizona Territory. What the legends and the movies don't tell us is that the "pioneers" were not simply agents of their personal destinies, for good or not so. The Clantons and the Earps represented interests who were vying for control of the land and its mineral wealth: the Clantons post-Reconstruction Southern Democratic forces, the Earps Eastern Republican business-men.

It was Josie Earp who lived the longest, dying in 1944, just two years before John Ford's *My Darling Clementine* was released and only eleven years before the television show—about what seemed so remote a past—that I watched as a child.

But even these words, fairly plain, tend to build a monument. A monument, too, is The Birdcage Theater, the only wholly intact original structure of Tombstone from those early days. For nine years, the theater, bar, gambling house, and bordello was open twenty-four hours a day. All of the famous were regulars, and Russian Bill, supposedly of royalty, who attended every night for two years until he tried to earn his unwarranted reputation as a bad guy by stealing a horse, for which he was hanged. And "Curly" Bill Brocius, who got shaves in a corner room with windows on the show, and was later killed by Wyatt Earp during the Vendetta Ride. Greats performed there: Eddie Foy of later Vaudeville fame, Lily Langtry, Bernhardt. (How worlds collide.) A poker game ran non-stop downstairs from opening to closing day, right outside the prostitutes' "crib," where Josie would receive Wyatt.

Now a museum of its past and of its former patrons, I arrive by serendipity just before twilight—the final and only patron during my visit. I have the building to myself. To stand in the middle. To perform my magic. When new owners took possession in 1934, and opened the theater for the first time since its closing in 1889, they found its contents undisturbed. Now, photos, guns, knives, paraphernalia, and old newspaper clips encircle me. The faro table where Doc Holliday played and sometimes dealt. The grand piano just feet away, and the space between, in which Holliday and Johnny Ringo held opposing ends of a bandana and drunkenly shot at each other, missing. The craps table. The stage. The twenty-six people killed there.

Just before she left me to myself, the guide who escorted me in drew my attention to the "birdcages" that ring the main room high above the floor.

"Those aren't theater boxes," she told me. "They're bordello rooms. Even the wallpaper, what's left of it, is the original."

For twenty dollars for the night, a man got a bottle and a woman. Maybe ten feet above the action of the gambling tables and the stage, he could drink and watch the activities, then without diffidence, draw the curtain. An act that intimate in a place that public, separated by only a curtain. So near in space, so far in nature. Like two events, two people, in the same space, one hundred and twenty six years apart.

So I have all the elements. It isn't hard. To see the crowded room. The cards. The dice. The theatrics on stage; the drama on the floor. Shots being poured. The shot ringing out. A shout. The general honky-tonk and the orgasmic grunts of hungry men from the cribs above. I can think it's all there in the space around me, an atomic-vibration off from the world I inhabit, events made material and permanent by the words that continually inscribe them. And then, I think, no, it is all long gone, the players forever emptied from that space. One man strikes it rich; another is murdered. A woman does what she must to survive. Some of it is remembered and talked about; some of it is not. But human time is not a compiling of moments, layer upon layer, like old newspapers there to be drawn from down in the pile. It is a fuse, burning up our moments as we live them, leaving behind its historical ash, but moving only forward, from opening to closing night, to another actor and another dusty wind, to me standing one day in the shadows, and beyond.

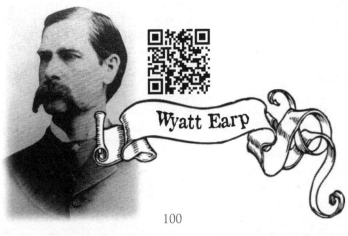

100

Arizona Ruins

LYN LIFSHIN

Past Mogollon River
      the limestone ruins
Scrape it with your finger
          and the floor breaks

               The tale
         must have dusted
     their dark
bodies as they squatted on these
      floors grinding
mesquite and creosote

No one knows
      where they went
         from the cliffs
    with their
        earth jars and sandals

Or if they
cursed the
      desert moon
         as they wrapped
their dead
     babies
        in bright cloth
          and jewels

2.

Now cliff shadows
      nest in the mud
         where the Sinagua
    lived
        until water ran out

High in these white cliffs
      weaving yucca and cotton
            How many nights did they listen
      for cougar
          as they pressed the wet
              rust clay
         into bowls
      They walked
200 miles to trade in Phoenix
      before it was time to leave

40 years
before Columbus

3.

Noon in the
caves

      It is summer
         The children are sleeping

The women
      listen to a story
      one of them has heard
      of an ocean

         Deerflesh dries in the sun
      They braid
willow stems
      and don't look up

When she
is done
      they are all
stoned on what could come
         from such water

It is cool and dark
            inside here

            This was the place

4.

The others
have gone to find
salt and red
            stones for earrings

            The children

climb down

            to look for lizards
        and nuts

        He takes the girl he
wants
        for the first time

            Her blood cakes
                    on the white chalk
floor

            Her thighs

                will make a bracelet
                    in his head

5.

Desert bees
      fall through the wind
           over the pueblos
                velvet ash and barberry

They still find

          bodies
      buried in the wall
              a child's bones
          wrapped in yucca leaves
            and cotton

Bats fly through the
      ruins now
          scrape the charred
     walls white

         The people left
     the debris of their lives here
arrows
     dung
         And were buried
    with the bright
turquoise they loved
    sometimes carved
into animals and birds

Goyathlay

DAVID S. POINTER

In 1906 or '07, my grandfather
traveled with his father from
Bates County, Missouri, into
Oklahoma Territory, seeing
Geronimo selling trinkets—
though I've forgotten what.
What I didn't forget was
that in 1909, the greatest
Apache guerrilla fighter
known to Mexican and
American man, died from
near-fatal car-crash-type
complications, and not
by way of Henry Ford
or Ransom E. Olds (REO),
but by falling from his
horse intoxicated at
almost 80 years of age
into a mud puddle.
After a lifetime of battling
both sides of border
oppressors, he'd been
understandably thirsty.

Geronimo

Magic Dogs

Native Americans were the first people on the planet ever to get a glimpse of a horse. When the first Native Americans traversed the exposed land bridge across the Bering Strait, they entered a land that had many strange and beautiful animals but no humans. These large mammals included mammoths, camels, saber-toothed cats, and prehistoric horses—tiny ponies that were no more than waist high. The same land bridge that allowed human beings to migrate into North America also let the first horses enter into Asia. The horses encountered by these first Native Americans were simply too small to be domesticated and ridden.

Ecological conditions on the North American continent quickly changed as the Ice Age ended and the glaciers retreated. The land bridge of Beringia sank back beneath the ocean. A large group of animals, specifically designed for the Ice Age, went extinct in the hotter, drier conditions. This included the tiny prehistoric ponies of North America. The ancestors of all modern horses came from a Mongolian horse, migrants from North America. It is ironic that Native Americans, the first people on the planet to glimpse horses, did not get a second look for over 15,000 years.

When Cortés landed on the shores of Mexico with an expedition that included 16 horses, these equines were the first to put their hooves back on the North American mainland. The De Soto expedition through the American south in 1539 was a disaster to all it touched, and an example of this failure was that, out of 214 horses that started with the expedition, only 22 returned. Some perished in battle, others from hardships, but many were stolen. Thus, the peoples of the Southeast became the first mounted Native American warriors.

In 1540, the Coronado expedition trudged into the American Southwest from Mexico City with an expedition that included over 1,600 horses. The expedition chronicler, a man named Castañeda wrote that many of the horses disappeared in the

vast Texas plains. Most experts agree that tribes of the Southwest—Navajo, Comanche, Pueblo, and Apache—started riding horses by 1550. By 1664, there were written accounts of the people of the Plains coming to the Southwest trade fairs with the intention of swapping captives and buffalo robes for horses. Their reputation on horseback and, most importantly, their reputation as horse traders, earned the Cheyenne the nickname of Painted Pony People. The oral traditions of many different Indian nations credit the Cheyenne with the introduction of the horse.

 For many peoples, such as the Sioux or Apache, the horse completely revolutionized their culture. The Lakota chief, American Horse, told the legend of the Thunder Horse. The Thunder Horse was a huge and monstrous beast that only came to Earth during the fiercest of lightning storms. While the tempest raged, the Thunder Horse would hunt buffalo, killing the shaggy beasts with a single blow of his massive hooves.

There was one summer that an entire village was in danger of starvation. All attempts to hunt game had ended in futility. A drought had left the crops parched and withered. The drought was ended with a terrible storm that filled the sky with thick black clouds, tornadoes, huge hailstones, and a thousand spears of lightning. The Thunder Horse dropped down in a terrible avalanche of speed, muscle, and fury. As the wind wailed with roars of thunder, the magic equine drove a herd of buffalo right through the center of the village, and the people were saved.

The only domesticated animals that Native Americans possessed before the arrival of Europeans were dogs, so perhaps it is only natural that the word for *horse* in most native tongues incorporates the word *dog*. The Snake called the horse "Big Dog." "Ponaka Nikita," meaning *elk-like dog*, was the Blackfoot name. The Sioux referred to the horse as "Shonka Wakon," or *Medicine Dog*. The Comanche showed their respect by naming the horse "Dog God."

A sad example of the importance of the horse in Colonial North America took place in 1698. Two Pueblo men were sentenced by a Spanish governor to be publicly hanged till death as punishment for the capital offense of horse thievery. Can you imagine being sentenced with execution for the crime of trying to steal, tame, and ride God?

Sources:
1. *Man on Horseback*, Glenn R. Vernam, Bison Books
2. *The Wild Horse of the West*, Walker D. Wyman, Bison Books

The Ballad of Pearl Hart

GARY EVERY

T he last days of the Wild West unofficially came to an end on May 29, 1899, when the Globe–Florence stagecoach was held-up by a pair of bandits. This holdup was notable for two reasons. The first reason was that this was the very last stagecoach robbery in the history of the American West. The second reason this hold-up was noteworthy was that one of the bandits was a woman—a woman named Pearl Hart.

Pearl Hart was born as Pearl Taylor in Lindsay, Ontario, Canada, in the year of 1878. After her career of infamy, a school chum wrote to the Arizona Historical Society and described the teenage girl he had known years before: "She was a pretty girl and had a wonderful figure and voice; could imitate a croaking frog, an owl, a hawk, could sing like a mockingbird; was lithesome, blithe, and witty; gushing with fun and jollity; also, a wonderful dancer, and very attractive. Everybody admired her and was proud of her acquaintance, but she possessed one detrimental fault that brought her many troubles. She was too amorous— accepted too many dates with handsome young men, which finally caused her undoing."

That undoing began in the shape of a young man named William Hart who married Pearl when she was just 16. William was not willing to work except to earn just enough to slake his thirst for alcohol. Rather than starve, Pearl hopped a train south of the border and eventually ended up in Phoenix, Arizona. While a resident of Phoenix, she made the acquaintance of a dancehall musician and tinhorn gambler named Dan Bandman. Dan taught Pearl how to drink, smoke, and even how to use opium. Their relationship was interrupted when Dan enlisted into the Spanish-American War.

For a while, Pearl made her living in Mammoth, Arizona, cooking for miners in a tent pitched along the shores of the San Pedro River, but soon, she made her way north to Globe, Arizona. It was while in Globe that she met her future partner in crime—a German named Joe Boot. When Dan Bandman reappeared on the scene, asking for money, Joe Boot helped Pearl drive her former lover away. Together, Joe and Pearl worked a small mining claim, but unfortunately, the ore was worthless. One day, a letter arrived from back East, announcing that Pearl's mother was gravely ill and that if Pearl wished one last visit, she had better hightail it back home soon. Desperate, Pearl and Joe came up with a plan.

On that infamous day, Henry Bacon was sitting atop the stagecoach as the driver. He had a Colt .45 revolver on him, but it was not loaded, as he did not expect to use it. The days of Indian raids and stagecoach robberies were long gone. In fact, the Globe–Florence line was one of the few stagecoaches that had not yet been replaced by the railroad. There were three passengers enduring the jolts of the rugged mountain road—a traveling salesman, a tenderfoot "with his hair parted in the middle," and a "Chinaman." As the driver approached the sharp turn at Cane Springs, he applied the brakes to slow down. As he did, two unmasked bandits leaped out from the bushes—both holding weapons.

The driver stopped, and the passengers exited. Although dressed as a man, it was obvious that the smaller of the two thieves was a woman. While Joe held a shotgun on the stagecoach passengers, Pearl searched the victims and put the money in a burlap sack. The salesman was carrying $380 dollars in cash; the tenderfoot, $36; and the "Chinaman," $5. The bandits took it all, plus the salesman's watch. As they prepared to leave, Pearl returned a dollar to each man, providing "just enough to eat."

Pinal County Sheriff, W. E. Truman, was soon hot on the desperadoes' trail and traced them to a schoolhouse twenty miles north of Benson. The posse snuck up on the dangerous duo while they were sleeping. A newspaper named *The Silver Belt* described their capture: "The officers came up, removed their armament and awoke them. The woman sprang up, fighting, but the man made no resistance. His companion reproached him in vile and profane language for his lack of sand and said that if the posse had tried to capture her while she was awake, she would have made some holes in it."

While in jail, Pearl became an instant celebrity. Again, *The Silver Belt* described the scene: "The woman is receiving much attention, an afternoon rarely going by without her having lots of callers and herself being photographed. The camera fiends have taken shots of her with all sorts of firearms and looking as much the desperado as they can make her."

The commotion in Florence was too much for Sheriff Truman to handle, and soon, Ms. Hart was shipped to the Pima County Jail in Tucson. A man named Ed Hogan, a notorious bicycle thief, who was serving a sentence for being drunk and disorderly, quickly befriended Pearl. Ed had nearly finished up his sentence and was a trusty at the jail. He fell in love with the female bandit, and she enlisted his aid in her escape. At night, Ed cut a hole in Pearl's plaster wall, but not before she penned a note that declared her a fan of the campaign for women's emancipation.

An editorial writer for the *Arizona Star* was impressed with her arguments. He wrote: "That laws should be enacted by the consent of the governed is a fundamental principle of our government. [...] Woman is not given the right to consent to the enactment of the laws that provide these penalties. Then why should she be made to suffer?"

The big city newspapers back east soon made the "Lady Bandit" a celebrity and a bit of a Robin Hood hero. Arizona newspapers and the law enforcement figures who had been forced to deal with her, replied that many of her troubles were of her own making, and even her own family was forced to admit publicly that Pearl was quite an opium fiend. Pearl and Ed ran off to Deming, New Mexico, where she had attempted to set herself up as a sort of queen of thieves. She was soon recaptured.

On June 15, 1899, Pearl and Joe Boot came up for trial. Joe pleaded guilty and was sentenced to 35 years in jail. Despite the hundreds of times Pearl had not only admitted, but even *boasted*, of her part in the crime, she chose this moment to plead her innocence. The jury came back with a verdict of not guilty. Judge F. M. Dean was outraged by this verdict and had the bailiff immediately arrest Pearl, while roasting the jury for their dereliction of duty. She was immediately tried again on the charge of stealing the stagecoach driver's pistol. This time, the jury gave her five years in prison.

Pearl was sent to the Territorial Prison in Yuma, and it was said that on her journey to her new residence, she puffed cigars constantly, emitting a stream of smoke that matched that of the locomotive she was riding. The celebrity circus continued. The guards "lost interest in watching the other prisoners and gravitated toward her cell with a hilarious enthusiasm that was harmful to discipline." There were also "visiting newspapermen and the camera fiends who always begged the warden to let her pose in the jailyard with a six-shooter or a Winchester." On December 19, 1902, two years before her sentence was up, Pearl was pardoned by Territorial Governor Brodie. The governor explained the pardon by stating that the Yuma Prison "lacked accommodations for women prisoners." Nearly half a century later, historian Bert Fireman uncovered the true story for the *Arizona Republic*. Pearl Hart was pardoned when the prison doctor confirmed that the female prisoner was pregnant. Rather than allow the scandal of a baby being both conceived and born in prison, Pearl was pardoned on the governor's sole condition that she leave Arizona for good.

After her release from prison, Pearl disappeared from certainty in the historical record. Some claim that she appeared on the Vaudeville stage

in a play about her exploits as the lady bandit in a show bankrolled by William Randolph Hearst. Others state that she may have briefly appeared in Buffalo Bill's Wild West Show. There were rumors that she ran a gang of pickpockets in Kansas City, while others place her in this fine metropolis but believe she only ran a cigar store while there. There was even one anecdote about a tour guide leading a group through the old Pima County Jail, when at the end of the tour, a little old lady came up and confessed: "Thanks for showing me where I stayed for a while. I'm Pearl Hart." Then, she walked away.

The last theories about Pearl Hart's whereabouts come from some old-time Arizona pioneers who believe that she settled down as a rancher's wife on a homestead outside Globe, not far from Cane Springs and the site of the stagecoach robbery that provided her moment of celebrity infamy. The woman who some believe might have been Pearl Hart passed away on December 30, 1955. But her legend never did.

Sources:
1. *Globe, Arizona*, Clara T. Woody & Milton L. Schwartz, Arizona Historical Society, 1977
2. *Good Men, Bad Men, Law Men, and a Few Rowdy Ladies*, John A. Swearengin
3. *Wild Women of the West*, Carl W. Breihan, Signet Books, 1982

Dingus

When Bloody Bill
Anderson was ambushed
out of his saddle, one of
his teen lieutenants, Jesse
James, got away, and after
the war, sometimes rode
for Confederate loans,
land-based and proper
over encouragement.
Pistols when pulled were
big as a Grey Ghost
battle flag, and when
the hardtack and luck
were good, the ex-guerrilla
could absorb even iron-
canister shot coated in
legend and blood, or
bullet hail hitting hard
as artillery projectiles.
Even after the failed
Northfield, Minnesota,
money run, Jesse and
Frank outmaneuvered
the thousand-man armed
manhunt failing to meet
the demands of original
hardcover-edition history,
full margins and mud,
home to Missouri, finally
back-shot on into world
literature and Western lore.

DAVID S. POINTER

Manassas

CATHERINE WARFIELD, 1816-1877

They have met at last—as storm-clouds
    Meet in heaven,
And the Northmen back and bleeding
    Have been driven;
And their thunders have been stilled,
And their leaders crushed or killed,
And their ranks with terror thrilled,
    Rent and riven!

Like the leaves of Valambrosa,
    They are lying;
In the moonlight, in the midnight,
    Dead and dying;
Like the leaves before the gale,
Swept their legions, wild and pale;
While the host that made them quail
    Stood, defying.

When aloft in morning sunlight
    Flags were flaunted,
And "swift vengeance on the rebel"
    Proudly vaunted:
Little did they think that night
Should close upon their shameful flight.
And rebels, victors in the fight,
    Stand undaunted.

But peace to those who perished
    In our passes!
Light the earth above them;
    Green the grasses!
Long shall Northmen rue the day
When they met our stern array,
And shrunk from battle's wild affray
    At Manassas.

The March into Virginia Ending in the First Manassas (July 1861)

HERMAN MELVILLE

Did all the lets and bars appear
    To every just or larger end,
Whence should come the trust and cheer?
    Youth must its ignorant impulse lend—
Age finds place in the rear.
    All wars are boyish, and are fought by boys,
The champions and enthusiasts of the state:
    Turbid ardors and vain joys
        Not barrenly abate—
Stimulants to the power mature,
        Preparatives of fate.

Who here forecasteth the event?
What heart but spurns at precedent
And warnings of the wise,
Contemned foreclosures of surprise?
The banners play, the bugles call,
The air is blue and prodigal.
    No berrying party, pleasure-wooed,
No picnic party in the May,
Ever went less loth than they
    Into that leafy neighborhood.
In Bacchic glee they file toward Fate,
Moloch's uninitiate;
Expectancy, and glad surmise
Of battle's unknown mysteries.

All they feel is this: 'tis glory,
A rapture sharp, though transitory,
Yet lasting in belaureled story.
So they gayly go to fight,
Chatting left and laughing right.

But some who this blithe mood present,
    As on in lightsome files they fare,
Shall die experienced ere three days be spent—
    Perish, enlightened by the vollied glare;
Or shame survive, and, like to adamant,
    Thy after shock, Manassas, share.

Small sacrifices

The winter leading up to the Battle of Thompson's Station was cold, and Theodore decided he could lose the two fingers and pinky toe. Their blackened color had frightened him at first, but now he'd become used to their ugly familiarity. Like an old, drunk friend who kept showing up for dates with your sister: his war scars were ugly and boastful and not going anywhere.

"My wife ain't writ for three weeks, Ted. Suppose she's dead?" Henry's voice split the silence. *Speaking of old, drunk friends.*

"Naw, Hank, but I suppose she supposes you are," Theodore replied.

The thought crossed his mind that his own wife might suppose both of the men were dead—heck, the whole bloody lot of them, as starved and frozen as they all were, sitting just outside Spring Hill. *Spring Hill*—that was a laugh. Nothing spring about it. The snow had killed as many men as had the last battle. He looked again at his fingers and could feel their searing death through his gloves. Merrily, his blessed wife and salvation for seven years, wouldn't find him as handsome with two fingers gone. He was sure of it. But he'd been looking for a way to get back home to her ever since the dreaded War Between the States began, and the loss of fingers and toes to frostbite might provide just the answer he'd needed for the past year away from her.

"Why don't you just write to Ann, then, Hank?" Theodore asked. "I'll transcribe it, if you tell me what you want writ."

A long silence passed between the men, and Theodore was well aware that Henry was concocting something. They'd known each other since childhood and enlisted together on a couple of straw feet when their family farms, sitting side by side in the lush fields of Tennessee, had come under attack by advancing soldiers. It was maybe the only decision Theodore had ever truly regretted in his young life, but Henry had a bigger regret.

"Suppose instead," Henry stammered, nearly afraid of the words that would leave his mouth, "you just write to Ann and tell her I've died?"

Another moment passed, and Henry was certain Theodore would hit him, maybe snatch away the bottle of oh-be-joyful, but instead an understanding reverberated between the two old friends.

"I could do that, Hank," Theodore replied, "but you'd lose the farm—"

"—I'd happily lose the farm if it meant losing her—"

"—and she's gonna need proof that you're dead. That ain't gonna be so easy as pennin' a letter."

"You could send her my ring."

"Yeah, but I mean *dead*." Theodore looked down at the ring Henry was sliding on and off his finger. *So easily.* There wasn't even a white line underneath the thing. Theodore hadn't been able to get his own ring off for years, even if he'd wanted to. Not that he wanted to. He wiggled the black, numb fingers of his left hand, and a thought throttled him. *It'd be coming off now.* "I got me an idea, Hank, to get rid of that woman'a yours who ain't worth shucks."

"Always appreciated your black little heart, Ted. Whatchya got?"

"Ain't my black heart; it's these black fingers." Theodore slid off his glove and braced himself for the smell that always followed. The moist lining of the leather glove had worn away to nothing, and from it spilled the stench of rotting flesh.

"Perdition, Ted! Why didn't you tell me?" The bottle slipped from Henry's grasp and spilled over his cavalry boots before he regained control of it. He couldn't stomach the rotgut with the new rot that filled the air. "You're gonna lose that whole hand if you ain't caref— Oh. Oh, I see." A smile lit Henry's drunken face. "Those black fingers look just about like they could fit this ring. Bloody shame about your fingers, though."

"Eh, small sacrifices I can muster. You do this for me, and I do that for you."

"And what am I doing for you, exactly?" Henry asked.

Theodore shrugged. "You take the fingers, you send me home."

"Home to your Merrily. That's all you've ever wanted. A way out of this war."

"And all you've wanted is a way to stay in it," Theodore chuckled. "So we both win."

"But you lose your fingers."

"And a toe." Theodore shrugged again and reached into his haversack for his razor and his leather shaving strop. "I was gonna lose 'em anyway. Might as well lose 'em for a cause." He handed the razor to Henry. "You're gonna have to do this, though; I ain't got the stomach for it. Cut up high. Get the whole thing, and don't leave no stumps."

Henry twisted the straight razor in his hand. "I ... I don't think I—"

"Tight lips, and do it. No Sunday Soldierin', y'hear? I just sharpened that thing last night. Ain't gonna get no sharper. What you drinkin'?"

Henry grimaced. "Some slush."

"Give it here."

Theodore splayed his left hand out over the rock he'd been occupying, finding a thick pile of fresh snow covering. His fingers were already numb, and the snow would keep the blood spurts to a minimum with the slower circulation in his fingertips. He looked one last time at his full left hand, chugged most of the remaining slush, and finished off the rusty, spoiled-citrus taste by inserting his leather shaving strop between his teeth.

"Make it quick, damn you," Theodore muttered over the piece of leather, and he closed his eyes and bit down, allowing the stale alcohol to run through his mind in thoughts of Merrily. *Oh, how he loved her. He'd be home to her soon. He'd be ho—.* Darkness consumed him before he had finished the thought.

Theodore awoke to war nurses making a fuss over him, bandaging up his fingers and toe, and Henry looming over him with pity. When the nurses had left, Henry extracted from his pocket a bloody linen handkerchief embroidered with his initials, and carefully unwrapped Theodore's fingers and toe. Encircling the blackened knuckle of the bloody ring finger, Henry had slipped his own wedding band in place of Theodore's.

"Perfect as can be, pal, except for your poor fingers," Henry said with a wry smirk, rolling the hanky back up and placing it in a small, wooden box with his soldier identification card and latest payroll stub. "They're writing up a Big Ticket discharge for that red badge of courage you got, but first, you gotta write to Ann for me and send this box along." Wiping his bloody hand on his wool coat pocket, Henry pulled out Theodore's wedding ring and slipped it on the injured man's right ring finger. "Merrily might still want you to come home with this, even if you ain't got the finger for it." He smiled, and, despite the obvious pain, Theodore smiled back.

"Find me a pencil," Theodore replied. By the time Ann would discover the coincidence between the box containing two fingers and a single toe and the fact that Theodore was missing those exact same two fingers and toe, Henry would be long gone. Theodore only prayed his blessed Merrily would be so happy to have him home that she'd forgive him the same coincidence. "And then, find me some more goddamn moonshine, so I don't look healthy enough to beat this letter home. I didn't just give you my ring finger for nothin'. I expect you to bring me some damn slush like a happy wife."

In the field where General Reynolds fell

(From the photograph by Timothy H. O'Sullivan,
Gettysburg, July 5, 1863)

General Reynolds isn't here now. Just six men,
nameless and dead on a sepia-stained field.

Stomachs, bloodied and bloated, push up toward heaven.
Hands splay next to heads like a motion of praise, forced

up by the bullets that laid them each flat on July's seared ground.
One man shelters his head with an arm angled

over his face, as if the last cannon's shot
hadn't already fired, their rifles been collected before them.

Now they wait with their ankles left out,
empty and pale below trousers rolled carefully up

by the same hands, maybe, that dragged their shot General away
on the first day of battle—only to come back, after,

to clean out pockets and bunch up socks on the feet of the fallen,
take their boots and their guns and their prayers

for those with more walking and fighting and dying to do.

KIRBY ANNE SNELL

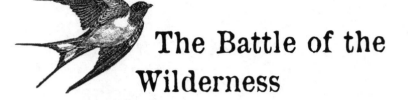

The Battle of the Wilderness

ELIZABETH ZUCKERMAN

His father would have taken Eli on these college tours, but when push came to shove, his father was in Berlin at a conference. So it was Eli's mother who loaded up the car for a few nights and drove Eli to Virginia, to look at William and Mary.

Eli resented this, in an irrational way that did nothing to decrease his resentment. In the first place, his mother had no business taking him to look at colleges. She, after all, had never gone to one. She had been a girl from a good-old-Virginia family who'd graduated high school solidly in the middle of her class, married his father about a month later, and set up housekeeping. When he was younger, Eli had gloated to his friends that *his* mother could always drive him *anywhere*. It had stopped being a bonus two years ago, when Kate, his first serious girlfriend, had heard him brag about his mother's supreme convenience. "My God, Eli," she'd said, staring at him. The lines between her nostrils and her mouth were deep, as if she had been trying not to vomit. "That's sick."

But here was his mother, sitting in the driver's seat as calm as could be, fiddling with the CD changer and asking him how he'd liked Swarthmore. "Good," he said, wriggling down into his seat until the back of his head was completely off the neck rest. "Nice campus. Their exchange program's okay, could be fun. Some of the girls are hot."

"That's the most important thing, of course," said his mother, smiling.

The smile made Eli want to sink even lower, to melt through the floor of the car and leave her driving on alone. *So embarrassing, my God. She doesn't even know what she's talking about. If she does this bonding stuff all the way down, I'm going to kill myself.*

Her Bob Dylan CD circled back around to the first track. Eli bolted upright and hit the eject button, cutting off Dylan's nasal voice mid-drone. "Switch time," he said. He put on Rihanna, which wasn't his favorite, but which he knew his mother disliked.

"Virginia's one of the most beautiful states," she remarked after a few moments, after just enough time had elapsed to register her distaste with the new music. "Be nice to go to college here. You could wake up and see this every day." She kept glancing over at him, checking for a reaction to her words. She'd been doing that a lot lately. It made him feel like a lab rat.

118

Eli leaned his forehead on the cold glass window. Trees flanked the highway like an honor guard. The sun was too bright and the sky too blue for him to see clearly what color green the leaves were. It was nice. He didn't think, in college, he'd do many tours of the landscape. "Yeah," he said. He put his seat back and closed his eyes.

"Hey, look at that," said his mother, some hours later.

Eli glanced at the car's clock—2:33.

"We're coming up on Chancellorsville. Want to stop and see it?"

His American History teacher had just finished with the Civil War. She taught a "greatest hits" class, focusing more on the fun stuff, like the actual battles, than on the causes of wars and their aftermaths. Kate had complained; Eli and his friends had been ecstatic. He'd liked it particularly because all those battles, the slow dragging tide of the war turning like a stiff wheel, reminded him that he was, in fact, a Yankee. He counted himself as one, anyway. He'd grown up in D.C., which was not—*not!*—the South. There was a difference. The Yankees had won. As, it seemed to him, they'd had to. Who could have beaten them? The South had the ridiculous romance, most of the best characters. They could keep it. They had lost; they needed something to cheer them up.

Eli had grown up thinking this, regardless of his good-old-Virginia grandmother and the grandfather whose hideous cracker name he bore; more importantly, he'd grown up believing it, believing in the pre-destination of the whole thing. But it had never had, for him, the apparently inevitable magnetism that still held sway over a quarter of the country. He said, "I'd rather just get to the hotel."

His mother swatted him on his bare, mosquito-bitten knee. "Honestly, kid!" she said. "Stonewall Jackson died here."

Eli remembered now. He'd liked Jackson, as much as you could like someone you only met through a textbook. He'd liked how scruffy the man had looked in the tiny picture the textbook's editors had granted him, how ordinary. He had ranted to Todd for five minutes straight about the stupid—*stupid!*—way Jackson had died. Or been killed, rather. Friendly fire, the Confederates themselves killing one of their greatest generals. "Fucking dumbasses," he'd said, suddenly furious without knowing why. "You act like that, you deserve to lose."

The sun shot straight into Eli's eyes as his mother took the exit to the site of the Jackson memorial. "Mom!" he said sharply. "Come on!"

"I want to see it," she said. She shot him a grin, one he refused to return—it was too conspiratorial; it made him too complicit in what she did. "And I'm driving."

Eli yanked down the eyeshade over his seat and hissed out his breath. He was not in the mood for something so horribly touristy, for fawning Southerners and silent homage. He wished he'd never heard of Stonewall Jackson, not if this were going to mess it all up. He didn't want to see a marble monument to The Hero's Eternal Greatness. That was wrong, all wrong for Jackson.

And his mother should know better. He was seventeen, about to go into his senior year in high school. She should know by now that there were some things in life that were special, secret. She should know that you didn't mess with them, that you left them alone, that they were all the more special because you didn't know why.

The gray humming highway had faded into a slender bumpy road, lined half with trees and half with dull little houses in gray and navy blue. His mother took a turn, and suddenly it was all green, the dull houses behind them, and in front and all around, only branches and leaves and a jolting unpaved path. The leaves were a bright middle green, a few shades lighter than plain-green crayon.

Down the path, he could see a small information center built like a rustic house, wooden and brown and showing its age, and a tiny parking lot. Maybe ten cars could have fit in it. It was empty.

Eli's mother parked the car and turned the ignition off. "We'll have it all to ourselves," she said. "Fun, huh?"

Yeah, great, I love to be alone in my misery. Eli swung himself out of the car. His father kept telling him he'd grow into his legs and shoulders. To this, Eli had only one question: *When?* He was getting tired of the abrupt slope of his shoulders, the way his arms hung limply at his sides like a broken puppet's; tired of the bony angles of his knees and the impossibility of looking good walking when his torso always lagged behind his determinedly huge stride. This time was no exception. His foot snagged on a sharp pebble just on the threshold of the little brown house, and he stumbled, his arms flying out wildly to stop himself from cutting his knee. His mother already held the door open; the sudden chill of air conditioning made him shudder.

"Whoa!" she cried, too loud, too strident.

Eli hunched his shoulders as he came into the information center, dimly lit and carpeted in some kind of nubbly red synthetic. The girl behind the counter—of course it was a girl; of course she was red-haired and attractive and about his age; of course she looked at him with a vague superior tolerance—was already giving his mother a few brochures. "We've got an exhibit just through that door on the battles that were fought here," the girl said. "Lots of photos of the soldiers, too—great pictures. And this." She opened out one of the brochures, printed in black and white on pale yellow paper, not glossy. "Here's a trail, if you want to do a little hiking. The memorial to Stonewall Jackson's about here." She tapped the middle of the circular trail.

Eli hated it when people used historical characters' full names. Thomas Becket, Susan B. Anthony, Stonewall Jackson. As if they could only recognize them by the entire name, as if they'd never cared enough to know them by one name only. He glared at the girl.

"Great," said his mother. "What do you think, Eli? Exhibit first, or trail?"

"Exhibit," he said. His mother loved museums. Maybe she'd take long enough that it would be too dark to hike the trail. He surprised a startled expression on the girl's face at his choice, and felt a flash of satisfaction.

He'd expected the display cases of artifacts from the war: minié balls, packs, rifles, facsimiles of letters in thin, unreadable cursive. The dark, curved wall hung with photographs of soldiers took him by surprise. All their eyes were deep and shadowy, from the fifteen-year old with shorn hair to the man of forty-nine, his beard outrageous and his mouth drawn downward. Eli's eyes flashed over the names; his mind lost them as soon as he'd read them. The names meant nothing. Their eyes stared at him, some impassive, some ambitious, some so very tired that it made his chest grow tight. He didn't look at dates of birth and death, both known and guessed. He didn't want to know. The fifteen-year old—a guess, maybe even younger, back then everyone had looked so much older than they were— gazed straight at Eli. *Here I am,* he said. *And there you are.*

His mother called his name from the other side of the curved portrait wall. Eli went to her, resisting the urge to glance over his shoulder and see who still watched him.

She was standing in front of a painting, romanticized but still hideous. The small canvas was filled with the yellow-tan color of scrub. Dark figures of men in uniform were frozen in contortions amid the dead bushes as explosions of fire burst all around them, arrested in motion. Eli stared, shocked. He didn't say a word, and when his mother finally did, it was in the hushed, reverent tone she used when she spoke seriously about the unknown future.

"Did you learn about the Wilderness in history?" she asked.

Eli shook his head.

She smiled slightly, a sad smile. "It was Grant's battle," she said. "Meade was still in charge, but Grant gave the orders. They fought it here, this area. Three days. At night, a brushfire started. They'd left the wounded on the battlefield, both armies. The men burned alive, and neither army could do anything about it. They just had to watch."

Eli's mouth was dry. He licked his lips, swallowed. "Who won?" he asked.

"No one. More Union soldiers died than Confederate, but Grant kept advancing. No defeated general had done that to Lee before."

He stared at her. "Where did you learn all that?"

"Your Gramma Sarah. She always missed Virginia after we moved. She would tell me about the war for my bedtime stories."

Eli laughed, the sound shocked out of him. "What happened to Cinderella?"

"Didn't exist," said his mother. "The war was much more romantic."

He looked at the painting. "Wow," he said. "That's ... not romantic."

She looked over at him, a strange softness to her smile. Eli realized, suddenly stunned, that his mother's eyes were on a level with his own. "I never thought so, either," she said.

He didn't argue later, when she suggested they hike the trail. Nor did he look at the girl behind the counter. It was a relief to step out of the air

121

conditioning and back into the warmth and faint moisture of the real air. Goosebumps broke out on his upper arms at the abrupt change, but they would fade soon enough. Eli rubbed his palms against his arms a few times, for form's sake, and went with his mother into those bright green leaves, walking on the brick path almost at her side. "Hike" was the wrong word for it, he decided. There was no challenge in the terrain. All flat, with a few gentle curves in the path, and some low stone markers.

His mother bent to read them aloud. "This is where Jackson's men got tangled in the brush. This is where the men were stationed who fired on him. This is where his horse bolted after they fired." Her voice was quiet and reverential without sacrificing any dignity. Eli tried to picture the scene, but there were too many trees, and the ground was too flat. How could a portion of an army have spread out here? How could anyone reconstruct it, here among this dizzying greenness, this enclosure, this place that clung to its secrets?

The monument was a miniature obelisk of graying stone, maintained by the local society dedicated to the memory of the glorious war. A short distance from it was a huge quartz rock, which, according to the information board, was the Jackson Rock. "The other generals put the rock there," his mother said, bending over the information board. "These are actually where he was first tended, not wounded."

It didn't matter, though, a little thing like that. Close enough. Eli could see it now. Jackson had been hit three times, twice in the left arm and once in the right. He could see the man, bleeding on the ground, red on green like Christmas. The branches would have hissed as Jackson's horse—Sorrel, he remembered—raced through them.

He knew it had been dark, but he couldn't banish the bright light of mid-afternoon. He couldn't make the colors dim. It had to be daylight, had to be open and obvious, had to be the thoughtless actions of true idiots that led to that horrible red and green. It wasn't fair otherwise. It was too easy to forget, in the dark, what a waste it had been.

By the information sign, his mother straightened up. Eli waited for her to turn to him, for the sad smile he was sure she'd be wearing. But she wasn't looking at him. She was looking at the small, green clearing, at the open spaces. She was a lone, distinct figure amid the green, her back unattended, vulnerable to enemy fire. It came to him as an edged shock that she must be thinking something, feeling something, and that her thoughts and feelings were as real and valid as his own.

Eli stood a few paces away, far enough from her that his thoughts didn't bump into hers. The distance between them hung slack, like a worn-out piece of elastic. He would have to pick it up and pull it taut again, if he

 wanted to come to her. Eli felt the bubble of silence swell around her, around both of them: fragile, glimmering with tears, waiting to be broken.

15 April 1865

R. JOSEPH CAPET

A shot rings out
like the chimes of the temples
in unconquered Hawai'i
or the snap of the bone
mere seconds later.

Well-rehearsed, the line
Sic semper tyrannis;
his one hope of acquittal wasted
on an illatinate audience.

For a hundred years
coins are minted and monuments built,
struggles for freedom staged
on the marble boards.

History goes on as it always has—
minding the crimes of its lowly actors
and peacefully forgetting
the deeds of great men.

Abraham Lincoln

123

The Exhumation of Abraham Lincoln, September 26, 1901

ROBERT L. PENICK

Gentlemen,
if you jostle my bones just once more
I'm going to shake the mold from these coatsleeves
and let that yellow bacilli drape its angry arm
around your heads. It's no good being moved so much
after death, starting with that hellish train ride from
Washington to New York to Indianapolis, finally to
Springfield, with Dr. Holmes embalming me every
twelve hours. No wonder I look so fresh: I'm as
well-preserved as the memory of a girl's first kiss.

Now, I long for darkness, the eternal black that wraps
the heart as well as the body in completeness.

Weld that lid on tight this time!
I am no longer fit for daylight.

Abraham Lincoln Walks at Midnight

(In Springfield, Illinois)

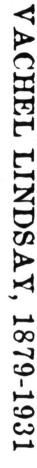

It is portentous, and a thing of state
That here at midnight, in our little town
A mourning figure walks, and will not rest,
Near the old court-house pacing up and down.

Or by his homestead, or in shadowed yards
He lingers where his children used to play,
Or through the market, on the well-worn stones
He stalks until the dawn-stars burn away.

A bronzed, lank man! His suit of ancient black,
A famous high top-hat and plain worn shawl
Make him the quaint great figure that men love,
The prairie-lawyer, master of us all.

He cannot sleep upon his hillside now.
He is among us:—as in times before!
And we who toss and lie awake for long
Breathe deep, and start, to see him pass the door.

His head is bowed. He thinks on men and kings.
Yea, when the sick world cries, how can he sleep?
Too many peasants fight, they know not why,
Too many homesteads in black terror weep.

The sins of all the war-lords burn his heart.
He sees the dreadnaughts scouring every main.
He carries on his shawl-wrapped shoulders now
The bitterness, the folly, and the pain.

He cannot rest until a spirit-dawn
Shall come;—the shining hope of Europe free;
The league of sober folk, the Workers' Earth,
Bringing long peace to Cornland, Alp, and Sea.

It breaks his heart that kings must murder still,
That all his hours of travail here for men
Seem yet in vain. And who will bring white peace
That he may sleep upon his hill again?

125

Big Daddy Joe

GARY EVERY

When the Civil War ended, there were lots
of newly freed *Negroes*
who were seeking a better life—
a home of their own,
a nest for a wife,
a sanctuary to raise children.
Some of the first working-class jobs
were on the railroad,
serving as Pullman porters,
graciously serving rich, curious travelers.
Railroads: the iron chain that bound the nation
from ocean to ocean—
after the nation nearly came apart
from internal strife and war.

Legend spread of the most famous of the porters:
Big Daddy Joe was so tall and strong
that he could change upper and lower bunks
at the same time,
flipping each bed with one well-muscled arm.
Once, he lifted a cowcatcher,
raising the front end of a locomotive engine
so a mother could whisk her baby
from the tracks
before the wheels cut her in half.
Once,
out on the vast stretches of the endless plains,
Indians attacked.
Fierce painted chiefs led bands
of Arapaho, Kiowa, and Cheyenne warriors,
charging toward the train.
Big Daddy Joe climbed on top of a passenger car,
and began to barter blankets and food
in return for safe trespass.
Imagine,
one of America's first working-class heroes
paying for a home to raise his children
(a house he never sees)
by traveling across the nation,
performing good deeds
all across the continent,
and his most famous act in battle
is the outbreak of peace.

126

At noon

we picnic in the cold.
Clouds roll in

on the park's western edge.
We view the spot

where a train twisted its way
down. Old 603

lives in a valley-grave.
See that girder bridge

off to the right. That's
where to look.

That awful night
she burned her way

to that very spot,
as metal and blood rained.

What's left is rust,
greened over all summer

with kudzu. But when
a storm begins—

clouds black as the steam
from that falling engine—

hail stones become
shards of glass.

HELEN LOSSE

Strathcona Park

PEARL PIRIE

this was all marine once. dig sand, hit veins
of shells that Rideau River doesn't explain.

the Epeiric Sea edged off. where's the bullseye
of when history starts. an arbitrary shot.

the river's swampy floodplain, or when it
was drained? when the flat banks,

the sandstone ripples were people with
the menfolk, musket crack shots,

when they caught blue herons, cranes,
and turtles home for supper. is work

the beginning of everything? so, mark
the spot becoming the Dominion Rifle Range

for the Boer War. hail Donald Smith,
the businessman who'd give more

bucks for bangs for his own regiment,
he who hammered the last spike of the CPR,

got the Honorific Lord Strathcona for a
(perhaps this will be redundant) horrific

war. how many board feet of young men?
7,894 killed in combat. twice that of disease.

double again for number of civilians.
quadruple that for young blacks interred.

but Donny was sworn into history, his namesake?
a 15-acre passage of gardens in 1904.

since then, Mathurin Moreau's English fountain
has flowed, egg and dart of beaux arts

with lion paws and maws. the war, like all wars
that parents us all, ignoring the peace between.

peace lets some ancestors and descendants
live. did this place begin when the walking garden

came in on gloriously dirty feet, transplanted
helleborine, speedwell, and lavender?

out of the cast-iron mouths of fish, water
to the cherubs and glyphs of seashells.

the swan ponds soon had their mouths filled with soil.
after WWII, not beauty, but economy, economy, my.

what won't be removed with time? groups lie in sun
in a gradient of skin. families fling frisbees

across racial lines. what good stays? this picnic table
is chained, for security, to the willow, presumably

in case someone would gaze at the tree like a tulip,
pluck it by backhoe force into private hands.

Lord Strathcona

129

Tower of London

LUTHER JETT

peel back seven
centuries of wallpaper.
blood soaks the stones beneath.

the upper chamber, dim
with dust, overlooks
the brown river broad as sky.

under the narrow window,
a stone basin, dry,
worn smooth by unknown hands.

dark raven—carrion bird—
cries on the broken wall.
the yard, paved with bones.

the throne's bare wooden
back, engraved with schoolboys'
rude initials—banished cushion.

a banner flies faded
by a thousand summers.
grass grows in the moat.

avoid the painted door,
the hollow staircase leading
past the iron room.

the redcoat sentry's
rifle shoots real bullets.
don't distract him.

Titanic

SEAN BRENDAN-BROWN

No romance in disaster, in
blanching alive when boilers
burst. Or blinded with grease,
screaming from a galley
where steam has peeled
the face from your skull;
bravery is tits on a boar
in an engine compartment
where a pipe-wrench swings
and a flotation vest is unlaced.

I think of John Jacob Astor
drowning in his favorite tweeds,
the platinum Cartier, a gift
from Edward VII, chiming half
of "Witch of the Air" before
freezing on its fob into
a glittering halibut rig; Astor
wasn't the type to save himself
with lipstick and a wig.

John Jacob Astor

The Titanic Disaster Poem

J. H. McKENZIE, May 1912

I.
On the cold and dark Atlantic,
    The night was growing late
Steamed the maiden ship Titanic
    Crowded with human freight.
She was valued at Ten Million,
    The grandest ever roamed the seas,
Fitted complete to swim the ocean
    When the rolling billows freeze.

II.
She bade farewell to England
    All dressed in robes of white
Going out to plow the briny deep,
    And was on her western flight;
She was now so swiftly gliding
    In L Fifty and Fourteen
When the watchman viewed the monster
    Just a mile from it, 'twas seen.

III.
Warned by a German vessel
    Of an enemy just ahead
Of an Iceberg, that sea monster,
    That which the seamen dread.
On steamed this great Titanic;
    She was in her swiftest flight;
She was trying to break the record,
    On that fearful, fearful night.

IV.
Oh; she was plowing the Ocean
    For speed not known before,
But alas, she struck asunder
    To last for ever more,
A wireless message began to spread.
    Throughout the mighty deep, it said,
"We have struck an iceberg, being delayed;
    Please rush to us with aid."

V.

The Captain, of the White Star Line,
  Who stood there in command,
Was an Admiral of seasoned mind
  Enroute to the western land.
The Captain thought not of his life
  But stood there to the last
And swimming, saved a little child
  As it came floating past.

VI.

Outstretched hands offered reward
  For his brave and heroic deed,
But the intrepid man went down aboard
  Trying to rescue a passenger instead.
This ill-starred giant of the sea
  Was carried to his grave;
On the last and greatest ship, was he,
  That ever cleft a wave.

VII.

Gay was the crew aboard this ship,
  Passengers large and small;
They viewed the coming danger,
  They felt it one and all.
On played the grand Orchestra,
  Their notes were soft and clear;
They realized God's power on land
  On sea 'twas just as near.

VIII.

So they played this glorious anthem
  Continued on the sea
And repeated the beautiful chorus
  "Nearer, My God, To Thee."
Then silenced when the ship went down
  Their notes were heard no more.
Surely they'll wear a starry crown
  On that Celestial Shore.

IX.

Colonel Astor, a millionaire,
    Scholarly and profound,
Said to his wife, "I'll meet you dear
    Tomorrow in York Town."
His bride asked a seaman true,
    "Oh say! may husband go."
The echo came upon the blue;
    He answered, "He may, you know."

X.

This man rushed not to his seat
    He seemed to have no fear,
Being calm, serene, and discreet
    Tendered it to a lady near,
"Oh go, he said, my darling wife
    Please be not in despair,
Be of good cheer, as sure as life,
    I'll meet you over there."

XI.

Well could he have known this dreadful night
    The sea would be his grave
Though he worked with all his might
    For those whom he could save.
This man a soldier once has been
    Of military art,
Proved himself full competent then
    To do his noble part.

XII.

Major Butt, well known to fame
    A lady did entreat,
To kindly name him to his friends
    Whom she perchance to meet.
He forced the men to realize
    The weaker they should save;
He gave his life with no surprise
    To the sea—a watery grave;
And with a smile upon his face
    He turned to meet his fate,
Soon, soon the sea would be his grave
    In and ever after date.

XIII.

And Straus, who did the children feed,
  Had mercy on the poor,
And all such men the world doth need
  To reverence evermore.
Oh, may the union of Straus and wife
  Be memorial to all men,
Each for the other gave their life,
  A life we should commend;
And may all girls who chance in life
  To read this poem through
Emulate the deed of such a wife,
  As went down in the blue.

XIV.

Down, down goes the great Titanic
  With faster and faster speed
Until Alas! there comes a burst
  She bade farewell indeed.
Farewell, farewell to land and seas,
  Farewell to wharves and shore,
For I must land beneath the breeze
  To reach the land no more.
I carry with me more human weight
  Than ever recorded before
To leave them on a land sedate
  They will land, Oh! land no more.

XV.

Only a few you see,
  May tell the story
Of this great calamity;
  Husbands, Wives, perhaps in glory
View the sad catastrophe.
  The Carpathia eastern bound
For the Mediterranean sea,
  Turned to the mighty sound,
The wireless C. Q. D.

XVI.

Quick was the preparation made
   To warn the unfortunate few,
For the homeless was cold and delayed
   Being chilled by the wind as it blew.
So to the youth
     Through life has started,
   Be ever thoughtful and true,
     Stay by the truth, be not departed
   Success shall come to you.

Oh, may you shun the Iceberg,
   By the dreadful work was wrought,
And prosper by the lesson
   This mighty ship has taught.

Sonnet IV

I shall forget you presently, my dear,
So make the most of this, your little day,
Your little month, your little half a year,
Ere I forget, or die, or move away,
And we are done forever; by and by
I shall forget you, as I said, but now,
If you entreat me with your loveliest lie
I will protest you with my favorite vow.
I would indeed that love were longer-lived,
And oaths were not so brittle as they are,
But so it is, and nature has contrived
To struggle on without a break thus far,—
    Whether or not we find what we are seeking
    Is idle, biologically speaking.

EDNA ST. VINCENT MILLAY, 1892-1950

Edna St. Vincent Millay

The Night Watch: Creativity in the Dim

HEATHER K. MICHON

Laura Cereta was one of those rare insomniacs who actually embraced her condition. She had been plagued with it since childhood, but as an adult she understood its merits. Her days were spent running a large and complex household, and she had come to realize: "I have no leisure time for my own writing and studying, unless I use the night as productively as I can."

"I sleep very little," she wrote to a friend. "Time is a terribly scarce commodity for those who spend our skills and labor equally on our families and our own work. But by staying up all night, I become a thief of time, sequestering a space from the rest of the day."

Cereta's juggling act would be familiar to any modern working woman trying to balance creativity with carpooling; yet she was writing these words in the late 1480s from the family estate in the northern Italian city of Brescia. Married at 15, widowed at 17, and dead at 30, her brief but intense career as a Renaissance humanist philosopher and author of some of the earliest-known feminist writings in European history was carved out in stolen moments in the flickering light of a candle.

The philosopher's *vigilae*, her "night watches," as she called them, may have been dictated by her situation, but a new study by German researchers indicates that Cereta's use of these late-night hours might well have contributed to the flow of her ideas.

"Darkness increases freedom from constraints, which in turn promotes creativity," writes Anna Steidle and Lioba Werth in the *Journal of Environmental Psychology*.

While organizational psychologists have studied the effect of many different environmental elements on creativity in the workplace—color schemes, spatial layouts, window views, even plants—comparatively little attention has been paid to light levels. Yet Steidle and Werth knew from other studies that, provided they feel safe, people tend to feel far less inhibited in darker environments. We're more likely to cheat on a game in a dark

138

room. We're more likely to hug or touch a stranger. We're more likely to divulge personal information. Maybe, they theorized, we're also more willing to take conceptual and creative leaps in the dark, as well.

In their study, the researchers broke student volunteers into three groups and exposed them to different levels of light: 150 lux (about the level of light on a very overcast day), 500 lux (the recommended lighting level for modern offices), and 1,500 lux (bright light). Before each experiment, the volunteers were asked to perform "priming" experiments, such as describing in detail the experience of being in a (safe) dark location or completing a word-search game full of synonyms for darkness. After about 15 minutes, each person was asked to complete a creative insight problem.

In six separate experiments, those in the most dimly lit environment consistently did the best, producing more creative responses to questions and drawing more vivid pictures of assigned topics. The researchers concluded that exposure to lower light did indeed elicit "a feeling of freedom, self-determination, and reduced inhibition," and that "overall, dim illumination and darkness induce a riskier, more explorative, and less vigilant behavioral style than bright illumination."

Perhaps, then, it's no coincidence that some of our earliest-known artistic expressions were drawn on the walls of deep caves. Human expression has always flourished in dim spaces—in large part because reliable artificial lighting has only been available for the past century. William Shakespeare may have composed some of his great works on a 100,000-lux summer's day, but he never stood in the lighting aisle of Lowe's debating the merits of LED over halogen.

Early modern literature owed much to the dark. In his 2005 study, *At Day's Close: Night in Times Past*, Virginia Tech historian, A. Roger Ekirch, notes that pre-Industrial Europeans used the night differently than we do today. People tended to go to bed shortly after sunset, sleep until around midnight, wake for a couple of hours, and then, return to bed for a period of "second sleep" until dawn. While the majority used the space between these first and second sleeps for activities like conversation or sex or prayer, by the 15th Century, a significant minority were turning to reading and writing to fill the hours.

Religious and social changes in the centuries after the Renaissance supported late-night creativity. The concept of silent reading, more suited to the night, began to catch on among the upper classes—Laura Cereta among them—in the late 1400s. By the mid-1600s, literacy rates had risen and the price of printed materials had fallen to the point where even laborers and servants could find pleasure in spending their nighttime hours with a good book. Catholicism had long supported the use of late hours for prayer and worship; the reading of the Bible and other religious texts and the rigorous self-examination demanded by the Protestant Reformation spurred the popularity of religious and moral texts, as well as the writing of journals, letters, essays and other contemplative writings ... many of which eventually found their way into print.

 At least one early Romantic poet found inspiration in the night. Edward Young (1683-1765) penned *Night Thoughts* in a series between 1741 and 1745 *(Night, sable goddess! from her ebon throne/ In rayless majesty, now stretches forth/ Her leaden scepter o'er a slumbering world).* Young is presumed to have written mostly at night, and even during the days, was said to have heavily draped his office windows at Oxford to simulate darkness while he worked.

Nocturnal creativity was not without risk. Before the late 19th Century, almost all lighting came from exposed flames, and there was a real danger to falling asleep with a candle or tallow still burning. And

 working in dim light led to long-term problems for early knowledge workers in the age before reading glasses. Samuel Pepys abandoned his diary at the age of 36 primarily because he feared permanent blindness from his increasing eyestrain. "My eyes, with over-working them," he wrote, "are sore as soon as candlelight comes to them."

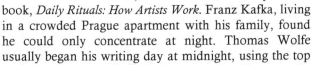

 Even as the world began turning into the industrial, brightly lit world we know today, some writers and artists held to the dim. George Sand wrote twenty pages a night for most of her career, having adopted the habit of semi-somnambulant scribbling during a youth spent caring for an ailing grand-mother, writes Mason Currey in his book, *Daily Rituals: How Artists Work*. Franz Kafka, living in a crowded Prague apartment with his family, found he could only concentrate at night. Thomas Wolfe usually began his writing day at midnight, using the top

 of his refrigerator as in informal standing desk (He was 6'6".). His typist began *her* day by collecting the sheets of handwritten text off the kitchen floor when she arrived in the morning.

Yet, not everyone has been a fan of night writing. "Never, never at night," wrote Günter Grass. "I don't believe in writing at night because it comes too easily. When I read it in the morning, it's not good."

W. H. Auden was a bit more blunt: "Only the 'Hitlers' of the world work at night; no honest artist does."

In their study, Steidle and Werth found that darkness enhanced creativity but was not conducive to analytical thought. It was in bright light where test participants found themselves best able to look at their creative bursts and ask the next logical question: is this new idea promising?

"Creativity may begin in the dark," they conclude, "but it shouldn't end there."

This is something writers and artists have long grappled with: the balance between conceptual leaps and technical finesse. Laura Cereta may have used the solitude of her dark *vigilae* to give voice to a new world where women were important and deserving of respect, but the ideas were formed from books and conversations and observations and meditations that occurred both day and night. Ultimately, the process of making our thoughts as perfect as possible is too complex to fit into the confines of a scientific experiment; we can only see the edges of it. Every writer has his own alchemical formula for creativity. We often spend a lifetime figuring out what it is.

LAVRA CERETA BRIXIENSIS.
LITERIS ORNATISSIMA

141

To the statue of Captain John Riley Parker on Lexington Battle Green Square:

LEAH ANGSTMAN

Forget the fife; forget the drum.
All's quiet now in Lexington.
Where war once raged and tore the Green,
The statue of Cap'n John Parker's seen

With musket clutched upon the thigh,
With Revolution in the eye,
With ammo' slung across the chest,
Tuberculosis in his breast.

Where troughs once wat'red horses' muzz',
Where cannon blazed and warnings buzzed,
Consumption c'not corrupt th' stone
Of Cap'n watching o'er his home!

From militia's French and Indian,
From Louisbourg to Abraham,
Capitulation of the Siege
Secur'd your place on New England's Green;

Elected by men of the town
To hold the Green and stand your ground.
Misnomered now as Minuteman
—Your men were not called Minutemen!—,

The militia's main was your command.
'Twas this militia'd take the stand
When swift you 'woke before the dawn
To answer the cry that 'coats had drawn

Upon your stead, your Green, your farm,
Upon your beloved Lexington!
Both sides were ordered not to fire—
Some unwisem'n disobey'd th' order.

None knows who fired that first ball;
But brave! The men did hear your call,
"Look up! Look sharp, Men; stand your ground!
Don't fire unless fired upon!

But if they mean now to have war,
Let it begin here!" your rally roared!
But one casualty did 'coats endure
'Gainst ten militiamen of yours

Emerged in lines from Buckman Tav'rn
And slaughtered there upon the Common!
Your cousin—bayoneted through!—
Slain but five paces 'front of you.

Yet, your revenge should Redcoats flee:
You'd follow them back to Boston's Siege.
You'd force them out! Your cousin 'venged!
Bunk'r Hill came, and Bunk'r Hill went;

The rest is history. The rest is known.
Consumption took you; your children grown;
Your farm passed on; your seeds all sown;
A mechanic's rest; your plow laid down.

This day in age: A hero unknown.
Yet, here you are, carved deep in stone.
Green on Green and readied with pride,
Your musket guards the Eastern side.

Sometimes at night, you walk the Lawn
And wait for warning's come by dawn
To sound the fife, to sound the drum
That all's not well in Lexington,

That if they mean war, it begins here,
But when you see all's well, all's clear:
You return to post, yet not to sleep,
But o'er the Eastern watch to keep.

143

Concord Hymn

(Sung at the Completion of the
Battle Monument, July 4, 1837)

By the rude bridge that arched the flood,
    Their flag to April's breeze unfurled,
Here once the embattled farmers stood
    And fired the shot heard 'round the world.

The foe long since in silence slept;
    Alike the conqueror silent sleeps;
And Time the ruined bridge has swept
    Down the dark stream which seaward creeps.

On this green bank, by this soft stream,
    We set today a votive stone;
That memory may their deed redeem,
    When, like our sires, our sons are gone.

Spirit, that made those heroes dare
    To die, and leave their children free,
Bid Time and Nature gently spare
    The shaft we raise to them and thee.

RALPH WALDO EMERSON, 1803–1882

Ralph Waldo Emerson

Letter from Thomas Jefferson to John "The Tory" Randolph— August 1775: A Revolutionary Poem

PHILLIP LARREA

Dear Sir—As to the violin left here in haste
Upon your urgent departure from our harbor:
I am sorry that our country's situation
Should render you no longer able to remain.
Though she is presently ill-tuned, and lacks a case,
I shall, with my utmost care, preserve her safety.

Upon arrival to your seat of government,
Please convey to your Ministry, this American
Opposition is no small faction, as believed.
They have taken into their heads, we are cowards,
And will surrender to an armed force. They are wrong.
This I affirm, and place my honor upon it.

If it be within your power to undeceive
On this point, at this critical time, you perform
Such service to nations, as the world has not seen.
They must hold out no false hope, no ignorance of
Our real intentions. Rather than submit, I would
Lend my hand to sink the whole island in the ocean.

As to your collection of law books: You may be
Willing to dispose of yours here, and replace them
With better editions. I should be happy to
Treat with you on this subject, in more peaceful times.
My best wishes for your felicity attend
Wherever you go. I remain your friend and servant …

Fourth of July Deliverance (After John Adams on Independence Day)

PHILLIP LARREA

Today I will sit on the ground beneath the overhang of this shady edifice in solemn devotion to sing sad songs for whom and what have died. Illuminating bonfires consumed, extinguished, or rather, vaporized once the precious case had been undone, pried open, left un-Locked. Even forever is a finite length of rope never long enough to prevent US all from hanging separately.

John Adams

146

Wrong, Right, and Reasonable

(Adapted from an essay
by Benjamin Franklin, 1767)

PHILLIP LARREA

It is Wrong, O ye Americans, for you to expect hereafter
That we will make any acts of Congress from the time we,
The Gentle Shepherd and his flock, get into power but such
As are calculated to impoverish you—and enrich us.
Our standing maxim is, you exist only for our sakes.
Your Lords we are, and slaves we deem ye.

It is Right to call this by the name "bounty."
We express our Goodness to you more clearly to intimate the
Great Obligation you are under for such Goodness.
Yet—you manifest the ungratefulness of your tempers by objecting,
In return for such Goodness, to take upon yourselves
A burden ten hundred times greater than the bounty!

It is Reasonable, O ye Americans, to charge you with dreaming,
Otherwise we cannot keep you so poor, but you may pay your debt,
Dreaming that you may encrease your own strength and prosperity.
Joseph's brethren hated him for a dream he really dreamed.
We, for a dream you never dreamed, which we only dream
You dreamed, have therefore resolved to hate you most cordially.

Benjamin Franklin

147

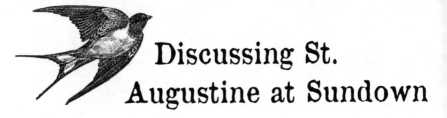

Discussing St. Augustine at Sundown

BRIAN LE LAY

Evil is an absence, you say, of good,
Of love for God, of daily prayer, not an entity,
Or our double lives merging like an inchworm,

Or dark ink spilled from a well onto a half-written letter.
Not that. The inexorable sin of stealing a pear
From a street market. Not the pear, either, or your hand.

At a table by the tall window, we marvel
At the soggy shriveled oolong tea leaves
In the black-ribbed cast-iron kettle

While across the street the second-story Colonial windows
With half-drawn shades stare down their brick façades
Like French waiters when a wine order is mispronounced.

In a few days, you'll return to your thin Japanese scrolls,
Platform bed under the window,
Which overlooks the long hedge

Where blackbirds hide from stray cats,
And strange black trucks with tinted windows
Spend the night. For now,

The corner monuments tell us,
Beginning with a curved cursive letter,
Each tiny grass stalk in the cobbled square

Sways with the soul of a 17th-century son
Who died for Massachusetts,
Bled out into the dirt like the last trickles

Of a dried-up river, buried
Under oak leaves and three feet of snow,
And no one knew where he had gone.

Beacon Hill, Boston

I go to work each day expecting joy.
This life's a dance, a romanced prance uphill
to scale new heights—a story scribed in stone.
Gaslight, dim as frozen ambered fossils,
weaves across crescendoed cobblestones
and, shaking off remembrance, leaves no trace.

DONOVAN WHITE

Top to bottom: 1.) Poet Oliver Wendell Holmes in Beacon Hill, 1893. 2.) Beacon St. in winter, c. 1897. 3.) Tremont House, corner of Beacon St. and Tremont St., c. 1828.

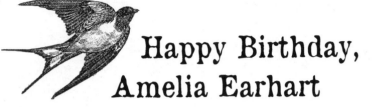

Happy Birthday, Amelia Earhart

ALEX STOLIS

The sea is resting now; birds circle quietly as waves simmer softly on the rocks. The sun arcs into a heavy cloud and somewhere here

is a woman who loves the water, loves the way the wind feels on her skin. She watches the blue change to gray to an off-white eggshell

and wants to paint it, capture it for her sons, for her yet-to-be-born grandchildren, even for the husband who doesn't notice how cracks

in the sky close for lightening. She knows the lure of flight, the lure of beauty, the possibilities that live in a moment. I want to disappear

in a green, green blade of grass, into a clear mist of rain, to the place on the beach where she rests her head.

Amelia Earhart

Eva

I never thought working at Photohaus Hoffmann would be so boring. In the three weeks I've been here, I haven't once been asked to get behind a camera, let alone in front of one. Instead, Mr. Hoffmann has me sifting through files and selling rolls of film. When important clients come in, he tells me to make them comfortable: to fetch them coffee, beer, teacakes, whatever they please. These clients are invariably fat old men from the National Socialist Party. None of them look all that important to me.

It's late, but I still have filing to do, and Hoffmann is expecting one of his important clients. He's given me a ladder so I can reach the files on the top shelf, and I'm teetering on its rungs like a ballerina. It probably wasn't a good idea to shorten my skirt before leaving for work this morning—I have a feeling the hem is uneven, and the amount of leg I'm showing is almost indecent. I hear a bell tinkle at the front of the shop, some manly murmurs and rustlings. I don't need eyes on the back of my head to see that Hoffmann's important client has arrived and that the two of them are settling down on the far side of the room, out of earshot but in view of the ladder, my legs.

I've been told that I have nice legs. My big sister, Ilse, giving me pointers on how to dress, says, "You're ten pounds too heavy, and your bust is small like mine, but as long as you're showing off your legs, no man will notice the rest." On the streetcar, men are forever brushing up against my legs or dropping coins by my feet so they can get a better look at me. It doesn't surprise me then, given the shortness of my hemline, to feel Hoffmann's important client staring at that part of me. Still, it's embarrassing to be looked at so intently when I don't know who's doing the looking. My face is bright red before I've even climbed down from the ladder.

They're standing up, crinkled and ungainly as a pair of elephants. The important client wears a pale English raincoat and clutches an ugly felt hat. He looks damp and smudged, with slick hair and a funny little square mustache. Though he isn't fat, there's something oddly soft about his body and the way his raincoat flares out at his hips.

"Mr. Wolf," Hoffmann announces his client, smiling like he knows something I don't. "Our good little Miss Eva!"

The men invite me to dine with them. I know this must have something to do with Mr. Wolf looking at my legs and that *no* isn't really an option, when it comes to important clients. Besides, it's late enough for dinner, and my stomach's growling from the smell of the beer and sausages Hoffmann got me to fetch from the corner pub. I guess it was a bad idea to skip lunch, diet or no diet.

At the backroom table, I'm aware of every clink of our cutlery, of the crawlings of Mr. Wolf's mustache as he chews, and the salty stink of the sausages. I try to keep my eyes on my plate, but Mr. Wolf is eating me up with his own eyes, which are the deep blue of mountain lakes, wild gentians. He has questions.

"How old are you, Miss Braun? Only seventeen? Good ... good. And where did you go to school? A convent? I should have known ... Convent girls have the sweetest manners. Miss Braun, do you like Wagner? You prefer modern music? Jazz? I'm afraid it's all primitive noise to me. You say it's fun to dance to? Far be it from me to keep a young girl from dancing! I imagine you are a very fine dancer, Miss Braun ..."

I don't know what to make of all this attention, and Hoffmann is no help. He listens on with glinting eyes and swills his beer, sitting back to belch and to feed Mr. Wolf the occasional tidbit about me: that I'm a fine little worker, that I've shown an interest in learning about photography, that he intends to let me do some modeling in the next few weeks—it would be a waste not to put such a pretty face to good use. They laugh at this.

They laugh at all sorts of things, like when I venture, "I'd like to do what Mr. Hoffmann does someday. Only, I want to take pictures of fashionable ladies, not politicians." I don't know what's so funny but laugh along with them anyway.

When supper's over, Mr. Wolf rises and smoothes down his raincoat, which he kept on all through dinner. Hat under arm, he reaches for my hand, tickling it with his mustache as he bends down to kiss it. The parting of his sleek, black hair is dusted with dandruff. "May I offer you a ride home, Miss Braun? My driver is just outside."

I cast a glance at the dark shop windows, the shiny black Mercedes parked outside them. "No thank you, sir. I still have some filing to do."

I'm clearing the table when Hoffmann comes back in from the street, shaking his head at me. "You really have no idea who that gentleman is, Miss Eva? No idea at all ... ?"

A few days later, a bouquet of yellow orchids turns up on my desk, together with an autographed portrait of Mr. Wolf in uniform. Mr. Wolf looks better in the portrait than in person. I can't tell if this is because of his uniform or Hoffmann's skill with a camera.

Freya, one of the other girls at work, pales with envy when she sees the flowers. "Oh, that man is a charmer! He must like you. I only got a portrait when I first started here." Freya is twenty-two and bosomy. Her hair is a few shades darker than my own. She doesn't have my legs.

I like to preserve the things I pick up from day to day, like theater stubs and calling cards and colored ribbons. I do this with Mr. Wolf's gifts, pressing an orchid inside my Bible and tucking his portrait away in the lining of my drawer. I know Papa wouldn't be happy if he found Mr. Wolf's portrait, and this is exciting to me. At the dinner table, when I ask him if he's heard of Mr. Wolf, he flares up instantly.

"That man? He's a dilettante, a fool who thinks he's omniscient. He thinks he's going to reform the world. Pah! I wouldn't trust him to run a classroom, let alone a country ..." Papa is a teacher and often speaks in classroom analogies.

Hoffmann has better things to say about Mr. Wolf. "He is a visionary," he tells me. "He is the future of Germany. You won't find a greater patriot, a better orator, a man of finer artistic sentiments! Consider it an honor, Miss Eva, to have caught the eye of a genius like him."

The more I think about Hoffmann's words, the more I believe them. In the darkroom, I'm haunted by Mr. Wolf's face swimming in red chemicals. I'm haunted by it drying out on the rack and glowering at me from newsstands as I shuffle to and from work. I'm even haunted by it when I look at my reflection—short curls, chubby cheeks, soft belly, nice legs—and try to figure out if I'm beautiful or just a convent-bred nobody.

When I'm invited to dine at Hoffmann's house, I don't expect Mr. Wolf to be there, and turn pink at the sight of him tramping into the dining room in his raincoat and heavy boots. As well as his felt hat, he's carrying a whip. His eyes goggle and moisten when he sees me, and he grips his whip tighter, licking his lips and rapping himself lightly on the thigh. I rise and present my hand to be kissed. Hoffmann's daughter, Henny, sixteen and seated beside me, does the same.

I'm glad to have Henny next to me at the table. We have a lot in common, and she's pretty in a thin-armed, gap-toothed way. Aside from her light eyes and freckles, she looks nothing like her father, with his drinker's flushed face and yellowy-white hair. Throughout dinner, we're able to avoid the talk of Hoffmann and Mr. Wolf by whispering and giggling together. I ask her what she thinks of Mr. Wolf, and she answers in a hushed, excited voice with something astounding.

"Evie, can I tell you a secret? He asked if he could kiss me once. It was a few years ago. I was in my nightdress."

I gasp. "Did you let him?"

"Of course not!" Henny cringes. "He's so *old*."

Across the table, Mr. Wolf is looking at us somberly and fingering his whip. I meet his gaze and feel myself blushing once again, regardless of how old he is. Hoffmann knocks back the contents of his glass and asks what we two little misses are whispering about.

"Clothes and shoes," we answer together, then collapse into giggles.

After a dessert of apple cake and cream, we filter toward the anteroom to say our farewells. I've already donned my winter coat and am brushing my lips to Henny's warm cheek, when Mr. Wolf appears at my elbow.

"Miss Braun, Mr. Hoffmann tells me you're planning on walking home in this cold weather. I won't have it. My driver will take you right to your doorstep."

I open my mouth to protest. I close it again. Mr. Wolf has already put his hat on and is offering me his arm. Under his other arm, he tucks his whip. As I link arms with him, Henny catches my eye over his shoulder and pulls a kissy-face.

Outside, a dapper chauffeur waits by the Mercedes, cap dusted with snowflakes as delicate as Mr. Wolf's dandruff. The driver salutes Mr. Wolf, who in turn raises his palm and says, "Good evening, Emil. Miss Braun would like to be taken home. She'll tell you where to go."

I hesitate, before deciding on a location far enough from my front door for the neighbors not to see. "Thank you. Take me to the corner of Elisabeth Street and Teng Street, please."

Moonlight stripes my sleeves as the Mercedes winds out of narrow Schnorr Street. I keep my eyes fixed on the back of Emil's head but can't help being aware of Mr. Wolf's sturdy presence nearby. I shiver involuntarily as a tramcar rattles alongside us on Norden Street.

"Are you cold, Miss Braun?" Mr. Wolf inquires.

"No, but thank you, sir. It's just that sound always spooks me. I'm sure it's what ghosts must sound like." I feel like an idiot for saying this, but Mr. Wolf chuckles warmly.

"You are safe from the ghosts with me, Miss Braun."

I never realized before how calming Mr. Wolf's voice is, low and slightly rasping. Still, it's not easy to feel calm with his blue eyes savoring me like I'm a slice of apple cake with cream. Gooseflesh tingles on my throat. When I breathe out, a cloud of mist follows.

At the corner of Elisabeth Street and Teng Street, the Mercedes comes to a halt. Emil steps out, and Mr. Wolf sidles closer to me along the leather seat. He takes off his hat.

My mind numbs. I think of what he asked Henny, what he's surely about to ask me. I can almost smell the sweet tea and apple cake on his breath, the foul base note of his saliva. The thought of saying *no* goes in and out of me like a swift, poisoned blade. I focus on his mustache.

Mr. Wolf bows to my hand. There's a tickle of coarse, black fur on soft skin, a puckered wetness on my knuckles. "Goodnight, Miss Braun. May we meet again soon."

In another instant, Emil is holding the door open for me. The cold is hitting my cheeks, and my heart is beating somewhere between my legs. I move my lips, but only the snow and stars can hear me whisper back to him, "Goodnight, sir."

I can see Mr. Wolf on the other side of the studio, leaning over Hoffmann's desk with a magnifying glass to his eye. In his baggy blue suit, he looks as lumpy as a sack of potatoes, yet there's something adorable about his form. I've already thanked him for the little box of marzipan fruits that he brought to my desk and the compliments that came with them. I've already offered him a taste of these fruits and watched as he lifted a tiny, perfect peach to his lips, observing sweetly, "Peaches and cream—just like your complexion, Miss Braun."

Now he's absorbed in business, and it's up to me to catch his eye before somebody else does. I rise from my desk and smooth my skirt, before clicking on my heels toward the filing shelf closest to Hoffmann's desk. Retrieving one of the files, I look askance at the men. Under the bright table lamp, they are murmuring over some prints of Mr. Wolf. I bite my lip. I let the file slip from my clasp and, with a gasp, bend to retrieve it. My skirt tightens over my hips. Their heads swivel.

"Miss Braun," Mr. Wolf says with a smile, "perhaps you can help us reach a decision."

"Yes, sir?"

"I always like to hear a lady's opinion on these things. After all, women are among my staunchest supporters." His eyes shine a deeper shade of blue as he says this. "Miss Braun, are you old enough to vote yet?"

"Yes, sir. I turned eighteen in February."

"Come closer, my child. Into the light. Good girl. And which of these men, Miss Braun, would you be most inclined to give your vote to?"

I can feel his eyes on the back of my neck as my short curls fall forward, blazing from brown to gold in the heat of the desk lamp. The same eyes bore into me from the photographs on the desk, making my breath grow shorter and my cheeks flare up.

"This one," I say, pointing to a picture in which he stares straight at the camera, as darkly enigmatic as a matinee idol. He's wearing a dark jacket and a National Socialist Party badge, which I know to be red, white, and black, though the photo doesn't show this. I've been given one of these badges myself but don't dare wear it, lest my father have a heart attack.

Mr. Wolf seems pleased with this decision. He takes a step back and inhales deeply. I'm afraid he can smell my moist, nervous heat, but if he does, it only pleases him further. "I agree, Miss Braun. You are very discerning." He steps forward again, glances down at the photo, and passes an unseen hand down the length of my body. "Mr. Hoffmann, be sure to make a copy of this picture for Miss Braun."

Back at my desk, I'm still tingling from his caress. I take a marzipan pear from the box and slip it into my mouth. Its sweetness sears my cheeks.

Braunhaus

The postman comes six days a week. I wait outside the gate for him, smoking against the wall and looking at the inky blue clouds, the pavement dappled with blue shade. Most days, my little sister, Gretl, waits with me, swinging her legs from the wall top and chattering on about her latest flirts. With Wolf away, there's nothing much to do but wait for news from Berlin.

It's summer, fine weather for waiting. Negus and Stasi start yipping on the other side of the gate as the postman nears our house, number twelve on sleepy Wasserburger Street. Wolf christened this place *Braunhaus* because of its cute brown-tiled roof and because it's a home for us Braun girls. He was the one who suggested I move Gretl in with me, so I don't get lonely out here in the suburbs when he's away on business.

The postman greets us both as Miss Braun. Like a lot of people, I don't think he can tell the difference between Gretl and me, so alike with our light brown curls and flowery dresses. As he reaches into the mailbag for our correspondence, I catch a whiff of sweat from his uniform. He hands me a wad of envelopes, and my hopes rise, then fall when I see there's nothing but bills and a letter from Herta, probably discussing her wedding plans.

"Nothing worthwhile," I sigh to the postman. I hand him a handful of coins and an eggshell-blue envelope to post to Berlin. It's the second such envelope I've given him this week.

I know Wolf doesn't have much time for letter writing, but is it too much to hope for a scribbled sentence or two? Wolf says that he has to be careful what he sends me, that his correspondence is constantly being monitored. If you ask me, he's just making excuses. Berlin is full of society girls, like that English Valkyrie whose legs he's always praising. It's no wonder he doesn't have time to write to me.

"Don't worry, Evie. Letters don't mean anything. It's better that he phones you," Gretl offers presumptuously.

It's really too much to be getting romantic advice from my little sister—a total fledgling, for all her flirts. "Oh, I'm not worried about *that*," I bluff. "I just thought he'd be sending me a check this week. He knows I wanted to order some new shoes to replace the ones Stasi chewed up." At this very moment, Stasi is sniffing at my cork-heeled sandals, her little black tail waving wildly.

Coming in from the garden, everything is dim and bloodless. "Liesl, bring some mineral water and apple juice upstairs to me and Gretl," I call to the maid, who's rubbing at some invisible blotch on the kitchen bench. "And set out some water for Negus and Stasi." It's almost midday, but we prefer to take lunch later in the afternoon on the flagstone patio, where we can play ping-pong and throw sticks for the dogs. Some days, it's all I can do not to swallow a bottle of sleeping pills instead.

I've stripped down to my bra and silk petticoat when Liesl comes up with a tray full of drinks and tinkling ice cubes. The dogs scurry after her, their black beards dripping, and spring onto the bed where Gretl sifts through my discarded outfits.

"... If Herta can't come swimming," Gretl says, "we should ask Marion. You know, I haven't seen her since the ball last month. Can I have this? You never wear it. Besides, I look better in burgundy. Evie, I wish you'd come with me tonight. Papa's going to give me an earful if I'm the only one. No, Ilse doesn't count. She *always* agrees with him ..."

As she talks on, I swivel in front of the mirror, sucking in my stomach so my ribs almost show. Wolf will probably complain that I'm losing weight, but if he cares so much, he can come home and buy me dinner at the Osteria every night. I shed my petticoat and reach into my wardrobe for a pair of light linen slacks, a black silk blouse to go with them. From the wall, Wolf's portrait sternly watches me dress. Again, if he disapproves, he should come home and do something about it.

While Gretl dines at our parents' house, I practice my yoga on the upstairs landing. I've been doing yoga for over a year and am more flexible now than I was as a chubby little schoolgirl, performing handstands in the convent gymnasium. I'm wearing a sleek, white leotard and balancing on one foot. I stretch my other foot up behind my head, so I'm poised in a sort of standing backbend. Gripping my toes, I fix my stare on a watercolor hanging in the hall. Wolf painted it years ago, before I was even born. It's while I'm in this position that the phone starts to trill. I drop my pose and hurtle toward my bedroom, catching the receiver midway through its second ring.

"Wolf?" I answer the phone breathlessly.

"Miss Eva! Get back to work!" Hoffmann blusters on the other end of the line, sounding as sloshed as usual. I wait for him to finish chuckling, clutching the phone to my ear and cursing myself for getting my hopes up once again. At last, the joke has run its course. "No, no, Miss Eva. Don't listen to me. But you have a television? Do your old boss a favor, and turn on the television."

"But it's all the way downstairs, Mr. Hoffmann ..."

"No buts, Missy. Pronto, pronto!"

I set the receiver down on the nightstand and scramble downstairs. The TV was another gift, like my dogs and ping-pong set. It's supposed to keep me amused at night but mostly just reminds me how dull it is around here. All broadcasts come from Berlin.

I kneel before the box and turn its dials, watching the screen flicker into life. Wolf is there in miniature, decked out in his clean-cut tunic, breeches, and peaked visor cap, and marching toward the Mercedes. He looks at once grand and diminutive.

"*Our Leader is getting into his car ...*" says the voiceover. "*... He is bidding farewell to the people. Their cries are thunderous as they strain to catch a final glimpse ...*" The camera pans over the crowd, who are cheering and saluting, their faces crumpled with an emotion that might be love, terror, or disbelief. There is a final shot of Wolf, standing in his Mercedes at the head of the motorcade. Then, the newsreel cuts out, and the night's programs begin: teenaged girls doing gymnastics in costumes as brief as my own. I turn off the television and rush back upstairs to the downturned receiver.

"Hello? Are you there, Mr. Hoffmann?" I can practically smell the smoke and booze on the other end of the line, listening to the background grunts of laughter. It's impossible to tell whether Wolf's laugh is among them. "Mr. Hoffmann?" I call again, more insistently.

My old boss' voice emerges from the smoke, so loud that I flinch upon hearing it. "Miss Eva! Isn't it wonderful? Like having him right there in the room with you!"

"It's something," I concede. I slip a cigarette out of the mono-grammed silver case on my nightstand and keep it poised between my fingers, unlit. Wolf hates me smoking and can tell when I am, even over the phone. "Mr. Hoffmann, is he there with you?"

"Our Leader?" Hoffmann bellows with laughter. "He's gone to the ballet with Lady Mitford!"

The Valkyrie. I sigh. As if there weren't enough legs to admire in the ballet. "When will he be back?" I inquire, blindly reaching for my lighter, which is also silver and monogrammed with a clover-like E. B.

"Ah, Miss Eva! You ask too many questions. No one can predict the comings and goings of our good Leader."

All I see is the blood of my shut eyelids, the white beat of sunlight overhead. I pluck a red grape from the fruit bowl. I crush it beneath my tongue. It's too warm and tastes ashy from my last cigarette. I think of the grape seeds sitting inside my stomach. If I were pregnant, he'd have to wed me. If I were pregnant, he wouldn't leave me for so many weeks. I touch the fabric of my flat stomach. If I were pregnant, maybe I wouldn't feel so empty.

Gretl is pinging the white ball against the table. The dogs are yapping and jumping to reach the hollow rattle. Gretl is determined to give me a headache, since I've refused to play stupid games with her. She doesn't understand that no amount of ping-pong or ball-tossing can make me forget that he's at the center of the world, while I'm stuck here in nowheresville.

The dogs are still yapping, though no longer at Gretl, when Liesl steps onto the patio in her sensible shoes and apron. "Miss Eva, you've got a delivery," she says. I look up, shading my eyes.

Gretl drops the ball and claps her hands, shrieking gleefully, "Evie, Evie! It's from Berlin! Open it; open it!"

The package is large, but when I knife it open, most of it's filled with red tissue paper. I toss the paper aside, letting the dogs run off with it in carnation-like bunches. Inside the box is a plush pelican with soft gray wings and cool marble eyes. I remember what they taught us at the convent about the piety of the pelican, nursing its young on its own blood. This isn't the first plush animal Wolf's given me.

"A pelican!" Gretl laughs and snatches up the toy. "How funny! Look at his big beak."

"There's also a telegram for you, Miss Eva," Liesl interjects, lowering her eyes and holding out a slip of paper. I don't give a damn if she's read it. I seize it as quickly as Negus and Stasi did the tissue paper.

The message is simple, but enough to have me leaping up from my recliner the moment I've skimmed it: *Leaving Berlin tomorrow. Braunhaus on Thursday. Love, Wolf.* All at once, the sun is beating to the rhythm of my heart. The sky is blue. The grass is green. I swoop the pelican up from Gretl's hands, examining its pretty eyes and wings.

"Well, what shall we call this fellow? Our Leader will want to hear its name when he comes by on Thursday."

I am preening on a rocky ledge beside the waterfall. Gretl is panting and splashing around in the foam. Marion soaks in the shallows, making circles with her toe on the water's surface. Though all of us brought swimsuits, we prefer to go naked. Midweek, we can usually count on this part of the lake being deserted.

Wolf doesn't approve of me sunbathing nude, but I'm sure he'd change his mind if he could see what a pretty picture we make. I'd like to take some pictures of Gretl and Marion, only my camera is all the way over on the shore, peeking out of my woven beach bag. Our picnic also waits onshore: fresh cherries and rye bread and flagons of sweet white wine. The only thing separating Wolf and me now is a day in the sun, a stretch of glittering water.

Wolf won't go near the water. He thinks it's shameful for a man his age to be seen wearing anything less than a two-piece suit or a uniform. "It is beneath one's dignity," he says. "Unless one is young and beautiful like you, my pet, one shouldn't be seen without clothes on." Even alone with me, Wolf refuses to strip past his shirt and socks. This is just one of the many eccentricities I must put up with, loving him.

I've already given Liesl instructions for tomorrow. In the morning, she'll clean the house and draw a hot bath for me with lots of scent and bubbles. After that, my driver will take her to Rischart for a Black Forest cake to serve with the cherry tea Wolf likes so much. Around midday, she'll set my hair and help me dress. I don't know what I'll be wearing yet, but will probably choose a pretty frock; Wolf loves seeing me in frocks, especially the kind with full skirts and modest necklines. For my nightstand, she'll get a bouquet of yellow orchids. My bed will be decked out with fresh silk sheets.

There's a rowboat bobbing on the far side of the lake, lacquered red against the pine-green waters. I squint and can almost make out the young male rowers, shading their eyes and squinting back at us. One of them points in our direction and calls something out, but his voice is lost on the air. I doubt they can see us any better than we can see them, and this makes me bold.

"Look out, girls. We have an audience!" I call to Gretl and Marion. Gretl shrieks and keeps thrashing about in the white water. Marion lets out a peal of laughter and stands up, a dripping blond nymph. She blows a kiss to the rowers.

I laugh, too, and slide back into the water as easily as a mermaid would, skimming the bottom of the lake until I reach the falls. When I surface at my sister's side, my heart is pumping, my face kissed by mist. Wolf says there's nothing more virtuous in the world than being young and strong and fair-haired. In this moment, I know exactly what he means.

Berghof

The price of having Wolf sleep beside me is waking to a bedroom that smells of sulfur. It's a price I'm willing to pay, squinting at the midday sunlight filtering through the silk curtains. Asleep, he looks less like a wolf than an old white cat, the kind you see dozing heavily on garden walls. He's getting older, and his dark hair has turned a mousy gray, shot with silver at the temples. Wolf likes to blame these silver hairs on his generals, who give him more grief these days than anyone else.

I sit up in bed, sheets bunched about my lap. I'd like to smoke, but of course, it's forbidden in here, more than any other room at the Berghof. There's a fresh, rotten smell from his side of the bed and he begins to stir, groping sightlessly for my thigh.

"My pet," he murmurs, or rather rasps. He's been calling me this name for years in private. In public, I'm still Miss Braun.

Wolf keeps his nightshirt on as he rolls onto me, raising my nightgown to my armpits. I accept his tight-jawed kiss and open my legs obligingly, wrapping them lotus-like around his back. I know many of the wives here make fun of my yoga and gymnastics, but they're just bitter frumps who walk around like they've got ice in their drawers half the time. Even with legs as limber as mine, however, it doesn't last for long. Wolf's love is like a fish leaping into a rowboat, thrashing for some moments, then sliding back into the deep, blue water.

He rings for breakfast as I repair to our bathroom, leaving the door open while I wash my insides with vinegar. Vinegar kills the stuff that makes babies. Wolf can't risk me having a baby, not while he's our Leader and Germany needs saving. When I emerge in my dressing gown, my hair is fluffy and golden and my face freshly scrubbed. Breakfast awaits us on the balcony: strong coffee and buttery bread for me; milk, cocoa, and chocolate biscuits for Wolf.

Wolf's balcony has the best mountain views in the Berghof and is off-limits to everyone but us. Sometimes, I imagine there are snipers in the mountains, but this thought doesn't scare me. If anything, I like the idea of being spotted breakfasting in the sunshine with the most powerful man on Earth. I could die happy sitting right here with Wolf.

He's dipping his biscuits in the cocoa, raising them to his lips with a trembling hand. Crumbs and droplets rain onto his nightshirt, soiling its white cotton. "Wolf, you're wolfing down your food again," I chide him tenderly. I reach out to brush some crumbs from his mustache.

He catches my fingertips in his mouth. "I'll wolf *you* down, my pet, if you're not careful."

I'm dressed for flower-picking in a peasant dirndl: frilly white blouse, red gingham bodice, full blue skirt, red-striped apron. Gretl and Herta also wear dirndls, in matching shades of red and blue. Gretl's apron is knotted to the left to show that she's single. Mine and Herta's are knotted to the right to show that we're not. Unlike Herta, I don't have a wedding ring. I do have a diamond wristwatch, which Wolf gave me for my birthday three years ago. I'm willing to bet I'm the only woman in Germany who wears her dirndl with a diamond wristwatch.

The irises grow waist-high and are a deep purple-blue, like Wolf's eyes. They smell soft and nice, like lipstick. When I bend down to pick the irises, their soft smell mixes with the damp of the soil. I gather them up in the crook of my elbow, angled skyward like a stage lady's bouquet.

The sun is already high, making my diamonds cloud over and my perfume melt away. Wolf's conference is probably close to finishing, and I'd hate to be absent from the terrace when he comes out, done with his boring business and ready to pay court to us ladies. One day last spring, I was late coming in from the meadows and found Wolf ensnared in conversation with Mrs. Propaganda. He didn't kiss my hand that day and gave her his arm when it was time to go in for lunch.

I turn to look at Herta. She smiles at me and nods, as if she's read my mind. Herta places a final iris onto her neat bouquet.

"Come, Gretl!" I call to my sister, who is further afield, sloppily bundling together as many flowers as she can carry. She turns around with a stupid look on her face, then gallops over, clutching her bouquet to her chest. Several flowers drop away as she runs.

We just have time to hand our irises over to the help and ask for some iced water, when Wolf's approach is announced. The secretaries who are smoking under the striped canvas umbrellas stub out their cigarettes, while Mrs. Propaganda and the other snobby wives herd together their children and start dabbing at their faces. Mrs. Propaganda has six perfect blond children, and Wolf admires her very much because of this. I don't know why this is such a big deal. If I had the chance, I'd give him twice as many children, better and blonder than hers.

Wolf steps into the sunlight, dressed in his gray uniform and military cap. We immediately draw in our stomachs and thrust out our chests, clasping our hands in front of our skirts and smiling prettily. Wolf walks with a slight stoop but looks happy, crinkling his eyes to smile back at us. His faithful Blondi is also happy, wagging her tail and strolling at his side. She sits down as he comes level with us, taking in our flushed cheeks and dirndls.

"What's this? Three maidens fresh from the fields!"

We titter appreciatively, though even Gretl is hardly a maiden anymore, nearing twenty-seven. "Hail, my Leader." I curtsy and present my hand to be kissed. He swoops down on it, blue eyes tugging at my own like magnets.

"Miss Braun, that costume suits you very well. But where are your little admirers?"

He means Negus and Stasi. "They're in my suite with Liesl, my Leader. I didn't want them running in the fields where there might be snakes."

"Mind *you* watch out for snakes, Miss Braun."

"I will, my Leader."

"That goes for all you ladies. Little Miss Braun, you're looking radiant, just like your sister."

Wolf moves on to Gretl, who curtsies and greets him with a squeaky, "Hail, my Leader."

After Gretl, he kisses Herta and the secretaries, then crosses the terrace toward Mrs. Propaganda and the other wives. He bends to kiss their hands and pinch the cheeks of their children—little girls in braids and frilly dresses, little boys in sailor suits or lederhosen. He gestures for the children to watch as Blondi performs her tricks: standing on her hind legs, turning in circles, howling like a wolf. Wolf joins in her howling and a child cries; the mothers laugh and clap their hands. The rest of us ladies start clapping with them. To applaud Blondi is to applaud Wolf, and Wolf thrives on being applauded.

We are standing outside the Teehaus, waving as the black Mercedes carrying Wolf and Blondi winds downhill into the low, golden sun. At this time of the day, Wolf always likes to be left alone, but that doesn't make me any happier to see him going. As soon as he goes, it's as if all the light has gone from the sky. The relief of no longer having to suck in my stomach and stick out my chest is also a deflation, as my body slackens like a punctured balloon.

But I did get some nice photographs today. Wolf walking in front with all the men. Wolf standing at the lookout with Blondi. Wolf inside the Teehaus, smiling down at his plate of cake as Gretl grins beside him, pretty in one of my old polka-dotted frocks. I try to take as many photographs as I can while Wolf is here, so I have something to calm my nerves when he's off touring Europe, making me crazy with fear for his life.

When all the fighting is over, Wolf says we can move to Linz together and live in a beautiful mansion, much more intimate than the Berghof. Only our best friends will visit us—no humorless generals or foreign ministers. He says that we'll marry and that I'll be his wife for the rest of his days, children or no children. He says that everyone will know the story of our great love.

For now, all I can do is keep him in love with me. I've swapped my dirndl for one of the fluttery tea dresses Wolf loves to see me in, white with blue flowers and a sweetheart neckline. As soon as we return to the Berghof, I'll start getting dolled up for dinner. It's late afternoon already and the sun is setting, almost touching the hazy blue mountains. Negus and Stasi seem intent on lingering, stopping to sniff every other pine trunk and wildflower.

"Evie, if you're not wearing the purple gown with the beading tonight, can I?" Gretl pleads, tugging on Negus' leash. Negus rears away from the buttercups he's nosing.

"I thought you wanted to wear the brown taffeta."

"I changed my mind. Please, Evie, please!"

"Okay, but if any of those beads come off ..."

"Thank you, Evie!" Gretl beams and winks at Herta. "Bruno says I look *en-chant-ing* in purple."

At the end of his leash, Negus has started sniffing again and is circling in the grass suspiciously. "Oh, no," Gretl pegs her nose with her fingers and turns away, putting as much distance between herself and Negus as she can. While we wait for Negus to finish his business, one of Wolf's adjutants catches up to us. He's a handsome, young man called Hans, who Gretl has been known to flirt with, though she's too embarrassed to flirt right now. Anyway, Hans seems more interested in speaking to me.

"Miss Braun, may I walk with you for a moment?" Hans stands up straight but looks nervous, eyes darting moistly from me to my companions to the path ahead.

"Of course!" I smile broadly and give him my arm, casting a glance back at Negus and my companions. "At this rate, we'll never make it back in time for dinner."

Hans smiles grimly and walks ahead with me a few paces, commenting on the beautiful weather and mountain air. His arm feels pleasantly muscular against my own, but I don't know what to make of it or the silence that comes over him once he's run out of small talk.

He clears his throat. "Miss Braun, our Leader has asked me to pass on a message. He says that your presence won't be required at the table tonight."

I should have expected this; Wolf's adjutants never come to me with anything but the news he doesn't want to tell me himself. All the same, my heart feels as if it's just been tossed off the top of a mountain. "Oh?" I manage.

"Our Leader sends his regrets. There have been some new arrivals, and only the officials and their wives will be in attendance. Of course, dinner will be brought to your suite at the usual time. And champagne, if you and your companions should desire it ..."

"Thank you, Hans. Tell our Leader I understand perfectly." I come to a stop and let my arm fall from his clasp. He salutes me.

"It has been a pleasure, Miss Braun," he says stiffly. "Forgive me if I've kept you too long from the other ladies."

"Not at all."

With a click of his heels, he sallies up the path in his smart uniform—just another man too honorable to acknowledge my existence.

Not a whiff of Wolf remains in my suite, which has been aired out and crammed with irises in crystal vases. I'm cuddled up on the corner of my sofa with my menagerie of stuffed animals. Among them is the pelican Wolf bought me when he was in Berlin five summers ago, a blond lion, a black bear, a green tortoise, and a silver wolf. I hug the wolf with one hand. I hold my champagne with the other. Herta stands by the birdcage, smiling and chirping through the bars at my pair of bullfinches. Gretl is sprawled on the floor in her stocking feet, flicking through movie magazines.

"Mwa!" She smooches a glossy photograph of Viktor Staal, looking stern and chiseled in a herringbone suit. "There's my future husband."

"He was very handsome in *Love School*," Herta agrees from across the room.

"His new film sounds so dreamy. Evie, can't you get us an advance screening?"

I roll my eyes and take a sip of champagne. "That's up to Mr. Propaganda."

"Ugh." Gretl wrinkles her nose, reaching for her own glass, which is perched dangerously atop a pile of old magazines. "I don't want to ask *him* for any more favors."

"As if you ever do the asking."

"Sourpuss." Gretl knows I'm in a bad mood but, as usual, won't let up. "It's only because you're so good at asking, Evie." She flips a page and has another thought. "If the guests tonight are movie stars, I'll just die."

"I don't think they're movie stars." Herta turns from the cage, hand on hip.

"Why not? Our Leader likes talking to movie stars."

"Hans said the dinner was for officials," I remind Gretl. "And our Leader is never as secretive about film stars as he is about politicians."

"Well, that's okay, then. I'd rather look at pictures of movie stars than listen to boring politicians."

Maybe I would, too, if I hadn't read all these magazines a million times, and if I didn't know Wolf would be there, at his most charming for the new arrivals. When I was a stupid little teenager, he used to put on his charm for me all over Munich, quite happy to be seen dining with a pretty, young girl. Now that I'm close to him, I have to stay hidden, though heaven knows I'm more elegant than I was back then. I'm the only woman in Germany who wears her dirndl with a diamond wristwatch, the only woman who's seen the view from his balcony.

Berlin

Wolf tells me not to come to Berlin. He tells me I'm too precious to set foot in the capital until it's been razed and built anew, with wide avenues and a dome bigger than any in Italy. It's not that long since Wolf was keeping me away from Berlin for other reasons.

"You're not made for society life, my pet," he used to say to me. "You're a delicate flower, and Berlin society is a dung heap."

I'm lifting dresses from my wardrobe and folding them into my open valise. I choose bright dresses printed with small flowers, polka-dotted dresses, dresses to remind whatever's left of society that it's spring, even if the sky is white with smoke and the trees are stripped of leaves. I choose dresses with starched cuffs and collars, which make me look younger than my thirty-three years. I choose a dress that's a favorite of Wolf's: darkest blue silk taffeta, embroidered with sequins. I call for another valise and haul my fox and mink out of the closet; furs are always elegant, and I don't know how cold it's going to be in Berlin.

The rest of my clothes can go to Gretl and Ilse, who'll need them more than I will. I've told Gretl to bury all of Wolf's letters to me. Though there aren't many of them, they're too precious to destroy or have anyone else read. Negus and Stasi are to stay behind in Munich; they could never cope with all the sirens and shooting that's going on in the capital. My parents say I should stay behind, too, but I know my place is with Wolf.

"He needs me," I insist. "And I can't very well abandon our Leader, after everything he's done for me."

Papa doesn't exactly approve of the things Wolf has done for me, but after all this time, he's resigned himself to them. I've spent half my life loving Wolf, living in sin for his sake, and there's nothing Mama or Papa can do to change this. In fact, I'd gladly tear the first half of my life away from them, if it meant giving those years to Wolf, instead.

On the midnight train, I travel north with the window shutters down. I don't believe in seeing more ugliness than I need to and prefer to keep the curtains closed, even when I travel by daylight. Cradled in my couchette, I let the train rock me deeper and deeper into my dreams of Wolf. Wolf victorious. Wolf asking for my hand in marriage. Wolf telling the world about our great love. When I awake just outside Berlin, there's nothing to see but dust above the city, and a platform crowded with deserters waiting to go south.

"My pet!" Wolf's eyes light up like a child's when I'm brought to his study at the Chancellery, a grand room done up in red marble with golden eagles perched above the doors.

I blush at being called this in front of the officers, who are grimly milling around the crimson tabletop. Wolf starts to get up from his armchair laboriously, but he's shaky on his feet these days, and I'm quick to fly to his elbow and help him settle down again.

From Wolf's desk, there's a view of the winter garden with its shimmering gray pond and heaps of dirty snow. Slumped in his chair, Wolf reaches no higher than the waistband of my skirt. He lowers rather than raises my hand to his lips, wetting it with his kiss and squeezing it limply.

"But, my pet, you shouldn't have come! It's not safe. You must go back immediately." His voice is no more than a rasping whisper.

"Nonsense, my Leader. I have everything I need right here." I smile down at him.

My luggage has been set down in the suite adjoining Wolf's apartment. Though the room is comfortable enough, I don't unpack—merely unlock my valise and select an evening dress to replace my traveling suit. As Liesl draws a bath for me in the red marble tub, I look up at the ceiling and listen out for the distant whirs and rumblings of the fighting outside. If I don't think about these noises too much, they're just a trembling in my blood, a shadow on my brain. They're a threat that can be lived with, like cancer or old age.

Wolf is turning fifty-six soon but looks closer to seventy, hunched beside me at the Chancellery dining table. I used to make fun of him for hunching like an old man, back when he was a vigorous fifty-year old. Now, it makes my eyes sting to think of how frail he is, the cruelty of those who've made him age so quickly. He eats noodles with tomato sauce. He gets flecks of sauce in his mustache, which I dab away discreetly once he's done with his plate. Everyone looks away, down into their champagne glasses, when I do this. I guess they feel guilty for taking so much away from him, speeding up his old age.

Before leaving Munich, I got Hoffmann to take one last portrait of me for Wolf's birthday. I've given Wolf self-portraits for almost every birthday since I've known him: he says there's no better gift I can give him than myself. In this portrait, I'm wearing a flowing white dress and looking soft, romantic, bridal. Someone has to remind Wolf that there's beauty in the world worth staying alive for.

My feet are planted firmly in the dust, set wide apart in their burgundy suede high heels. I'm not cold, though the weather is raw, and my coat is flapping open at my knees. The gunfire in the east is closer than it was a few days ago but sounds softer through my earmuffs, as I narrow my eyes at the empty champagne bottle. The pistol was a gift from Wolf: small and serviceable, perfect for a woman. I squeeze the trigger, and the bottle shatters at the neck, its green shards the only bit of spring in the garden.

I squeal and clap my hands, calling across the courtyard to the secretaries, "Did you see that? Right in the throat!"

By the doors to the Chancellery, men in uniforms mount guard. Mrs. Propaganda smokes between them, broad-hipped and immaculate in her white suit and pearls. She arrived here with her children a few days ago and will be staying with us until the end. She told me as much herself. Now that all the other wives have fled south to their country houses, Mrs. Propaganda sees fit to confide in me.

When she heard that the secretaries and I were going out for target practice, Mrs. Propaganda said coolly, "I'd rather shoot myself than even set eyes on a Russian soldier."

I actually agree with her, but either way, I think it's best to be a steady shot. Besides, it's a good way to pass the time while I wait for Otto to move my things down from the fractured Chancellery building and into the shelter below ground. There were air raids last night, and it's now possible to see the heavens from my suite.

I hand the pistol to Miss Christian, who steps forward and takes aim. At the same moment, Otto emerges with four leather valises piled up in his arms, followed by Liesl, who bears a pair of matching hatboxes.

"Miss Eva, are you ready to go down?" Liesl's high voice carries through the open air.

"Just a moment, Liesl." I smile and gesture at Miss Christian and the bottles.

Miss Christian pulls the trigger. Another champagne bottle shatters, sending shivers up my spine. She turns around, flushed and grinning, and hands the pistol back to me. Its weight is warm and small in my clasp, like one of Blondi's newborn puppies.

The other secretaries coo with admiration. "You did it! You shot him dead." When a bomb thunders somewhere to the east, not one of us flinches.

I place my pistol in its case: elegant and silver, lined with velvet, engraved with my signature E. B. Tucking the case under my arm, I turn to Liesl. "I'm ready. I guess we'd better go down, if we want to make it to the underworld in time for tea."

Otto leads us out of the winter garden through a damp, narrow corridor. His shoulders are broad and tense under his uniform shirt; a young man's shoulders, not at all like Wolf's. At this time of the afternoon, Wolf will probably be down in the kennel, cuddling the pups and talking to them in a voice so whispery only they can hear it. Now that so many of Wolf's men are fleeing Berlin, dogs and women are his only comfort.

Passing through the cellars, I spy case upon case of champagne; enough to last us all a year, even if we're never sober. The pantries are stocked with canned fruit in syrup, canned tomatoes, cans of rich black caviar. When we reach the metal door that opens to the underground staircase, we're greeted by armed guards. They ask to see our papers.

For him, I am descending to a place that the bombs can't touch, a place where night and day are the same, and where I will always be loved. The guards step aside. Before me, the ground opens up.

LYN LIFSHIN

Seeing the Documentary of the Liberation of Bergen-Belsen

The bodies like driftwood
tangling, naked. Pale
as marble or roots of
trees suddenly torn
from the earth that
held it like the
scalped shrunken head
of the Polish scientist
who tried to run,
unreal as the man
shot when he chewed
earth to get out of
the cell for air, the
bottom half of his body
burning. Bodies stacked
like wood, a cross
dangling, child frozen
into a breast, his
legs cut off, wrinkled
little hot dogs.

No Pasarán!

LUTHER JETT

You stand blocking
the doors to your palace
with mile-wide shoulders and
brass sleeves—knives
for smiles and guns for a handshake.

Grimacing, your mild voice thick
with venom, you say
it's all been said that can be said.
And there are no new territories
to light out for, no eyelands
green, untrodden.

No entry is your password, no
regrets, you shrug, and turn your back.

But I am History,
with my frayed, damp cuffs,
my undimmed eye, my lonesome teeth.
And I will wait here by your door,
with my broken songs, unfinished,
waiting only to be written down.

And the stars
reel in their orbits round
some pole that neither you
nor I can reckon. Stranger!
Do not ask to know—
the final line has not yet
been crossed.

FEATURED WRITER

Jesseca Cornelson, an associate professor of English at Alabama State University, is currently working on a book-length collection of documentary poems based on Alabama history. Her critical work appears in *The Great Recession in Fiction, Film, and Television: Twenty-First Century Bust Culture*. Her poetry has recently appeared in *Cellpoems, Salamander, Platte Valley Review,* and *The Dead Mule School of Southern Literature*. She is looking forward to upcoming residencies at the Sundress Academy for the Arts' Firefly Farms and the Catskill Center's Platte Clove Reserve. She keeps company with two adventure hounds and enjoys

Jesseca Cornelson

hiking and kayaking in Alabama's stunning natural spaces. Four of these poems are based on documents. "Subject: Scene Description" and "Subject: Autopsy Protocol" are found poems from the coroner's notes on the death of Michael Donald, who was lynched in her hometown of Mobile, in 1981. "Lynchable Offenses in Alabama, 1889-1920" is drawn from a record of lynchings compiled by the Department of Records and Research at Tuskegee Institute. In these poems, all words except those italicized are selected from the documents in the order in which they appear. "Iberville at the Mouth of the Myssyssypy," however, is a liberal reworking of entries from the journal of Pierre Le Moyne d'Iberville, published as *Iberville's Gulf Journals* by the University of Alabama Press in 1981.

Fragment of the Lament of Young Wives Abandoned

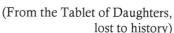

(From the Tablet of Daughters,
lost to history)

. . . . of unstoried name,
who comes from the *dark earth* by the water's edge,
who set my name aloft . . . whisper on the water's edge.

From the time he brought me leaves for brewing
and a small pot made of fired clay, the meat of . . .
. . . .

[Fifteen and twenty and more] men *could not hold*
the sleek backs of my love surfacing over me;
Fish he became, a [school of fish], the whole ocean's *Ark*.

Swarming my skin, . . . *many, an array of himself.*
The mouth of evening swallowing the sun
changes color before spitting out cooling stars.

~

By these banks my feet have plodded through dark mud.
. . . . . . cursed the slender rows of stalks, floods
and the man who left, wearing *on his back* [my skins]
. . . only coming home to leave again.

O mother, how can your voice match those of [morning birds]
while your daughter . . . . . .
What man did you [*tender* me unto] . . .
For what price did . . . . . . ?

. . . . . . [*pantries*] well-stocked [at least],
your robes silk, and does Father sleep on feathers?
If my *voice* might still reach [you, come *be*] by my side.

Poem in the Voice of the Poet

i.
Returning with a bespectacled gaze,
I dissect even my family as I pathologize

the past, outdoors only a vast specimen
to photograph, report to my colleagues up North.

ii.
Here, on barbed wire, a shrike has thrust
a horned beetle, shelled in inky iridescence,

like oil and rain on asphalt, the spectrum
bottom-heavy with blues and violets,

only a wild bleed of yellow and red at the fringe.

iii.
In Canada, studying French, I had my parents
mail me hot pickled okra. Each year in Ohio,

I cooked greens, calling home to check the recipe,
the kind without measurements, the kind

cooked from the memory of a big table set
years ago by a grandmother for her sons

and their children, the sweating glasses
of sweet tea tasting too much like well water

for a child's taste, garden okra fried dry
in a grainy crust, onions and cucumbers

in vinegar and water, everything only salt,
pepper, sugar, and sometimes bacon

or ham hock. I studied in Columbus
instead of coming home for Mawmaw's funeral.

What do I know of family now but Christmas Eves?
Between stories of shipyard injuries,

legs welded clean off, falls from scaffolding
that burst organs like ripe fruit,

I joke of calluses from grading.
And now to find home, I thumb brochures,

visit archives, read journals of the long dead.

Poem in Which She Imagines the Voice of History as a Grandmother

Listen, baby, I know you wish
this was just some fitful sleep

and a caress from me could rest
the thoughts that keep you tossing,

your hair sticking in flat curls
against a brow gone cold with sweat.

I know the *shush nows* you want whispered,
the dreadful stories you think you've dreamt

and want me to untell.
You think you're sitting at my feet

like when you were a child, and I'd read
the Good Book to you? You think the stories

I got to tell come down a mountain on stone
or are some secular reckoning

of who lived, who died, and why? Ain't no why.
You know that. Us versus them;

oldest story there is. This is what
you've always done. Your fingers know *grab*.

Your teeth know *bite*. The fight in you
comes first. You make a story later.

The worst blood is in the memory.
The story is to make it mean something,

to make that blood come out in the wash.
But listen to yourself. I'm only

the voice of you who lived.
I'm how you haunt yourself.

White Ghost

Just some ancient government surplus
gone sad little militia group, whose frayed

canvas and gaunt whiskers ramshackle a woods,
bound by too loosely strung barbed wire

and creeks that run as they want.
Just the stammering absurdity of a cabin lit

by Coleman lantern and the clank of steel
letters shaped in negative as they hammer

inky ribbons. Just a ghost with such
ribbons for hair, speechless save

for the smudges that dog her, howling
in silent typescript. Are they tendrils

or contrails, the manifestos that coil
from her skull, still smoldering an ire

that disappears in air? Wonder at the soot
on hands that tried to catch her, lips

that tried to say, *Wait. Please. You needn't
hate your way through the hurt.* Who

can say but the un-oiled hand-crank
machine and the ache that resonates through

its weary body, a hollowed metal drum? Who
can say what the words are that will wake us,

leave us as ourselves and not some tired
iteration the past would have us be?

Postcard of Certified Live Birth

From the thirteenth of one month to the third
of the next, I was a legal no one, birth uncertified.
A photocopy on bond paper—legal green—proves
my father was a carpenter *(Usual Occupation:*
Self-Employed), that of *Children Previously Born*
to This Mother none *are now living, were born alive*
but are now dead, or were *born dead*. Under
Signature of either Parent, the loops of my mother's name
are fainter, rounder than the signature I'd later copy
for school excuses. Four unknown names in dated scrawls
keep it company. The typed *j*, *e*'s, and *s*'es
of my father's name are tucked inside my own.

Iberville at the Mouth of the Myssyssyppy

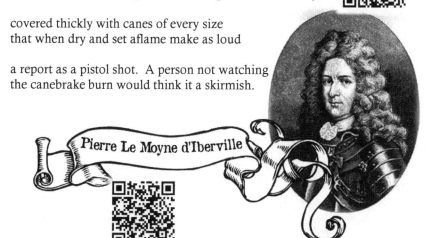

(Adapted from the March 1699 entries
of *Iberville's Gulf Journals)*

Under the fog, the river swells with uprooted trees,
but the wind has gone to some other place.

With two canoes, my brother and his men stalk the shore
where yesterday an Indian abandoned a fire.

Such strange trees, with leaves fat as hands,
rise with the ground as we go—fruitless, offering

nothing. Even seaside blackberries were yet green,
weeks away from being ripe enough to eat.

I fired two canister shots from the swivel gun.
All this land is a country of reeds and brambles

and tall grass in a ground inundated a foot deep
as far back as half a league. This is impenetrable country,

covered thickly with canes of every size
that when dry and set aflame make as loud

a report as a pistol shot. A person not watching
the canebrake burn would think it a skirmish.

Pierre Le Moyne d'Iberville

177

The South, as if Translated from the Japanese

Let every
white petal
admit guilt

~

Hardy yellow pines
loblolly and slash and shortleaf—

Not violets at twilight
but weedy wisteria

clambering up trash trees
the long-fingered limbs

of mimosas and trees of heaven
mob the roadside

honeysuckle past dark
windows rolled down

the dark fragrance
the departed leave

~

Silver King by the bushel
fat flats of strawberries

whole backs of pickup trucks
laden with baskets of tomatoes

or swollen-bellied watermelons
parked beside county roads

always a hand-painted sign
leaning against a wheel

~

Nothing like the sandy soil of a ditch
for blackberries to rise up

out of the disappearing hands
of white ground-borne flowers

Subject : Scene Description [Re: Case No. 01(A) 81-30941; Michael A. Donald, Subject]

Attend time and date hours,
for the rigor is easily broken.

No slight history
was found hanging

by a rope
from a tree.

The scene is vacant,
barely.

The ligature is a classic
hangman's noose.

The rope above the head
is looped around the tree

and tied in a bowline knot.
The boy has the following clothing:

a blue warm-up coat,
a gray sweater,

a brown checkered shirt,
a T-shirt,

a pair of blue jeans,
a pair of white

jockey shorts,
a pair of white

socks, and a pair of
Converse high-tops.

The feet barely touch the ground.
The legs are slightly flexed.

The left side of the head is up
and the right side down.

The left arm is flexed
almost across the abdomen.

The right arm is flexed
slightly with the hand dropped.

The feet barely touch the ground.

Subject : Autopsy Protocol [Re: Case No. 01(A) 81-30941; Michael A. Donald, Subject]

("The autopsy protocol is the written record of
the objective observations. ... Careless use of
language can provoke unnecessary questions."
—Vernard Irvine Adams,
Guidelines for Reports by Autopsy Pathologists)

An autopsy is witness
to the body,

to the cheeks and chin, clean shaven,
to the confluent lines forming V's,

to abrasions extending over regions
in brown-blue herringbone.

The greatest press upward
over the right;

On the left,
bloodtinged

lips are swollen.
No swelling

of the neck
will be described.

This wound involves skin
over the joint, tendons exposed.

A classic hangman
loops around the coils.

The ligature measures
the neck beneath the knot.

Right the neck,
for no vessel is greatest.

The right hand
stabs the left.

The air contains blood.
The heart weighs free.

The stomach contains
pieces of orange.

The architecture
of the dark is exquisite.

Evidence graphs blood.
Contents of pocket:

a watch and chapstick.

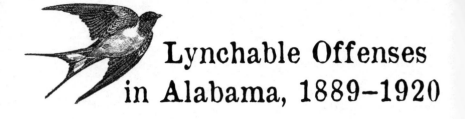

Lynchable Offenses in Alabama, 1889–1920

(According to the complete record of lynchings in
Alabama from 1871 to 1920—compiled by Monroe M.
Work, Director, Department of Records and Research,
Tuskegee Institute, at the request of Marie Bankhead
Owen, Director, Alabama Department of Archives and
History—from 1889 to 1920: 240 black men, 33 white
men, 10 black women, one white woman, and one
man, race not given, were lynched in Alabama.)

Murder, *of course, and* rape,
robbery and miscegenation,
but also being a desperado,
incendiarism, testifying
against whites, being an outlaw,
arson, barn burning, political
activity, alleged arson,
giving evidence, burglary,
incest, turning state's evidence,
passing counterfeit money,
elopement with a white girl,
being mistaken for another,
murderous assault, giving
evidence against "White Caps,"
paying attention to a white girl,
accomplice in a murder,
being unknown in name or offense,
mistaken identity, race prejudice,
rape *and* murder, complicity
in a murder, robbery *and* shooting,
criminal assault, dynamiting,
insulting white woman,
attempted attack on woman,
murder of deputy sheriff,
being whipped by landlord
Sam Spicer and out of revenge
later shooting Mrs. Spicer,
being half-witted and frightening

women and children near Birmingham,
burglarizing a store, shooting a white man,
dangerously wounding a Deputy Sheriff,
poisoning mules, being released
on bail, robbing a store, highway
robbery *and* not giving enough of road
to white men *and* being insolent,
making unruly remarks, being reported
to have fired a gun and boasting
of getting a policeman, killing an officer
of the law, not reported, having killed
a policeman, raping a six-year-old girl,
murderous assault on white woman
and having a father accused of rape
of same white woman, insulting
a woman, striking a man with iron
pipe and fractioning his skull.

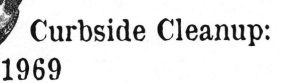

Curbside Cleanup:
1969

DAVID S. POINTER

President Nixon's motorcade
rumbles along Truman Road;
Kansas City motorcycle cops
process the street next to Cash
Bargain Lumber Company; I'm
the astonished 7-year-old kid
holding historic hedge apples—
I might've averted Watergate
with one light-green diplomatic
greeting missile, misshapen,
splatting up a sidewalk balk
over the smoked glass non-
transparency entrusted with
the gigantic peoples' planet.

The Diabolical Voodoo Experiments of Harry Smith, Folk Music Anthologist

ED HAMILTON

Harry Smith lived in a tiny, junk-filled room in the Chelsea Hotel with no kitchen and a bathroom down the hall. This was where, in inadvertent homage to the Collyer brothers, he stored his vast collections. Filling most of the floor space, and rising up toward the high ceiling, were stacks of brown cardboard boxes and jumbled towers of books, magazines, and records—some of which had collapsed into heaps that spread out across the floor. A single bed piled high with blankets and clothes, a pair of straight-backed chairs, and a table heaped with papers, dirty dishes, cameras, tape recorders, and film-editing equipment, competed for the remaining space. There was a small, rust-stained sink and an ancient, groaning refrigerator in one corner of the room.

Not to overlook the Satanic altar. For as Harry was an artist, and as art is a kind of alchemy, it should come as no surprise to learn that Harry, the Renaissance man of the art-drenched Chelsea, was also a master of the occult. The makeshift altar, fashioned from a small rickety desk, was festooned with foul relics and grisly power objects, fetishes and totems made from hair and bone and beads and cloth, from scales and fur and tattooed human skin. And it was over this very altar, on a moonless night in 1965, that Harry, together with Leticia—his most trusted assistant—were bent in rapt absorption. Upon the altar, ringed by votive candles, lay a mangy tomcat, his gray fur flecked with pet cemetery dirt, his muzzle stained by dried blood and gore that had oozed from his mouth and coagulated beneath his head. As the pale, black-haired, hollow-cheeked Leticia dripped blood from a decapitated chicken's neck onto the corpse, Harry intoned the time-honored mystical words: "Rise, Fluffy, rise!"

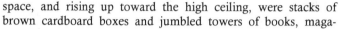

The Chelsea Hotel was a ready vessel into which was decanted the zeitgeist of the sixties, the result of which was a non-stop, 24-hour orgy of art, music, literature, dance, and free love, fueled by powerful psychotropic drugs. Often described as "Victorian Gothic," the crumbling, gabled, red brick pile on Manhattan's 23rd Street had been a haven to the arts since 1884, housing such luminaries as Mark Twain, Sarah Bernhardt, Thomas Wolfe, and Dylan Thomas. Basing its construction on the principles of French utopian philosopher Charles Fourier, the architect Philip Hubert designed the hotel as a socialist experiment in cooperative living. And now, some eighty-odd (and I mean *really* odd) years later, it were as if the experiment had gone awry and the overgrown Petri dish had spawned a strange and beautiful monster.

Of all the hotel's inspired, eccentric, and downright mad denizens, no one individual more fully typified the wide-open spirit of the Chelsea experience than the infamous Harry Smith. Painter, filmmaker, folklorist, collector of pop-culture ephemera, and counterculture jack of all trades, it was Smith who compiled and edited the *Anthology of American Folk Music*, so influential to the generation of folk singers who congregated in the bars and coffee shops of Greenwich Village. Short and slight, bearded and gnome-like, Smith was a sawed-off plenipotentiary of the demimonde, gathering around him through the force of his personality a misfit crew of disciples and sycophants to aid him in his seminal work. Progress on his various projects, as one might expect, was sporadic at best.

"Rise, Fluffy, rise!" Harry repeated. "Rise, Fluffy, rise!!!" Harry and Leticia chanted in unison.

Nothing happened.

"Drizzle some of that blood in his mouth," Harry suggested.

"Good idea," Leticia replied. "Hold his mouth open."

And as Harry used his sacrificial knife to pry open the cat's stiffened jaws, Leticia redirected the flow of blood, pinching the chicken's neck to titrate the amount, onto the appropriate area.

Still nothing. The blood sloshed off the cat's face to no effect.

A woman in her early thirties, Leticia Skankmeyer had been working with Harry for a little over a year. Her father, having set her up in the Chelsea because it was less expensive than the mental hospital, had provided her with a generous allowance, which she used to keep Harry in cigarettes, liquor, and film stock. Gaunt, skeletal, with heroin tracks and suicide scars on her bony arms, Leticia had filled in her pale, hollow cheeks with white pancake make-up, completing her ghoulish look with black lipstick and eyeliner. She wore black leather pants, stretched tight to her frame, and, in a nod to her feminine side, a frilly purple blouse. Despite her otherworldly appearance, Leticia was primarily interested in film. She and Harry had taken a break from the grueling editing work on Harry's great magnum opus, *Mahagonny*, to embark upon this experimental foray into the realm of Voodoo. Leticia was plainly in love with Harry.

"I don't think it's working," she said.

"Nobody asked you," Harry replied. Raising his arms heavenward, he danced about the room, chanting vigorously, evoking the spirits of the goddess Erzulie and the powerful snake god Damballah Wedo—and knocking over several stacks of books and records in the process.

Harry's appearance was no less shocking: He had splotchy skin and bad teeth, and the dark circles under his eyes were accentuated by his Coke-bottle glasses. His long, unkempt hair and beard were flecked with gray, and his bony hands with their long, dirty fingernails were stained yellow from nicotine. Stooped and with a slight hunchback, Harry wore ratty, thrift-store clothes—a white shirt yellowed with sweat and the pants from an old gray suit. Though he usually topped this outfit with a threadbare black trench coat, for the ceremony he had donned a beige bathrobe adorned with alchemical symbols. He did not reciprocate Leticia's affection.

Giving up on the dance, a winded Harry poked the cat with his finger: "Snap out of it, Fluffy. What's wrong with you?"

"It's getting smoky in here from all these candles," Leticia said. "Can I open the window?"

Harry, who was becoming increasingly frustrated, did not acknowledge her. Instead, he redoubled his efforts: "Arise, foul beast! Up! Up! Rise, Fluffy, rise!" He paused to observe the effects of his words, then said, "Shit, you goddamned cat, get up!"

"I don't think he's gonna rise, Harry."

Harry grabbed the cat and tried to stand him upright. The dead animal tottered briefly, then fell back over.

"He's stiff as a board," Leticia observed.

"Pull his tail," Harry commanded. "Tickle his foot." Leticia did as she was told. "Give him mouth to mouth."

"No way!"

"Stick him with a fork."

Leticia found one in the sink and jabbed the cat fiercely several times, making a mental note to bring her own silverware the next time she dined at Harry's place.

"I've seen the Mambo High Priestess do this a dozen times," Harry said. "And with people, too! Grab that candle and singe Fluffy's fur! That'll teach that lazy-ass cat."

Leticia grabbed a nearby candle from a pile of boxes and swung it toward the altar, inadvertently brushing into Harry's bathrobe. The highly flammable fabric burst instantly into flames.

"Shit! Goddamn! Get some water!" Harry yelled, as he struggled to get out of the burning garment.

"Oh, my God!" Leticia panicked, grabbing the nearest thing—which happened to be Harry's urine pitcher.

"No, not that!"

But she had already sloshed him with the foul mess—which also contained the contents of an ashtray. At least it put out the fire.

Sputtering and shaking piss and cigarette butts from his face and hair, Harry said, "What the hell is your problem?"

"I told you no good could come of this," Leticia said, still brandishing the pitcher. "You have to use the bathroom like everyone else."

"But it's a mile down the hall!" Harry whined.

At that moment, the door burst open, and a man bounded into the room, almost causing the two sinister celebrants to jump out of their skin. It was Chuck McGillicuddy. Obese, baby-faced, with a wisp of a beard, Chuck was a young wannabe Hell's Angel who had been drummed out of the novitiate for unknown offenses. He now lived at the Chelsea and worked as Harry's bodyguard, cameraman, and factotum.

"Harry! Harry!" he cried out excitedly.

"You idiot! Don't barge in like that!" Harry screamed. "Now, look what you've done! You've spoiled the whole ceremony. Thanks to you, Fluffy will never chase mice again. I hope you're satisfied with yourself."

"Sorry," Chuck said, eyes downcast.

"Stand over there out of the way until we're done." Harry knocked the papers off a chair and sat down. "I don't understand it," he lamented. "I did it just exactly like Mambo Ethyl taught me."

"Maybe we need a fresher cat," Leticia suggested. "This one's been dead for a week."

"What's the point, then?! Then I'm just like a doctor or something lame like that!"

"No, you're not, Harry! You're a genius. Everybody knows that."

"If I can't even raise a cat, how am I ever supposed to raise a human?" Harry said, burying his head in his hands in despair.

After a time, an impatient Chuck asked, "Are you done?"

"No," Harry said. "Wait a minute." Then, after a pause, he added, "All right, what is it?"

"There's a huge party up on the sixth floor! You gotta see it. It's great."

"Don't go up to that stupid witch's party!" Leticia snapped.

"What? What are you talking about? What witch? How come nobody ever told me about her?" Harry was irritated to hear that he had competition. "Well, there you have it, right there. My magical aura has been disrupted by the presence of a contrarian force. No wonder we can't raise this damn cat." He rose from his chair with renewed purpose. "Well, we'll see about this."

"Forget about that dirty witch," Leticia said, desperately jealous. "Let's try with a fresher cat. I know where there's one on the ninth floor, and maybe it's in the hall right now."

"A freshly dead one?"

"No, it's alive. At least, the last time I checked," Leticia admitted. "But that shouldn't be a problem. It's a small one, and I think it's been declawed."

But Harry was fixated on the more vexing question of the new witch in the building. "I seriously doubt she's a real witch," he said, "or else I would have sensed her presence."

"Oh, she's a witch, all right," Chuck assured him. "And by the looks of her, a powerful and charismatic one."

"A horrible, wicked, *ugly*, old witch," Leticia said. "Let's not go up there, Harry."

190

"I don't know about the *ugly* part," Chuck said.

But Harry had already made up his mind. He pulled off the urine-soaked bathrobe, wadded it up, and tossed it in the corner behind a pile of rubbish. He donned his grubby trench coat, then grabbed Fluffy by the legs and tossed him to Leticia. "All right, get this down to your freezer. We'll raise Fluffy later."

"Why do I have to keep him in *my* freezer?" Leticia protested.

"Because I have ice cream in mine, okay?"

This cat's no good anyway, Leticia thought, but she knew from experience that further argument was useless. When Harry wasn't looking, she slung the stiffened feline out the window onto the roof of the building next door.

Revelers were spilling out into the marble-tiled hall on the sixth floor: beatniks in their existential black, folkies in their flannel shirts and pageboy hats, mods in miniskirts and paisley jackets, hippies with their long hair and beads. Even a couple of weirdos in business suits. All seemed to be in uncommonly high spirits, getting along famously despite their differences.

"What's wrong with these idiots?" Harry asked, scowling crossly. If there was one thing he couldn't stand, it was people having fun. Especially in *his* building.

A drunken, wild-haired Gregory Corso stumbled up to Harry and his friends. "Hey, man, where's your invitation?" he asked Harry jokingly.

Harry, who had never liked Corso, discreetly kneed him in the groin. "That'll put a damper on his evening," Harry said, as the beat poet collapsed to the floor in agony.

 In more ways than one, the Australian artist Vali Myers' Chelsea Hotel apartment was as different from Harry's dingy crash pad as day is from night. Spacious, bright, and airy, with several large windows facing 23rd Street, it was actually a suite consisting of two rooms and a kitchen. Vali had been in residence for a scant three months, and already she had taken major steps to make the place her own and to fill it with her carefree spirit. She had painted the walls canary yellow with a bright red trim, and the ceiling green with a red and yellow sunburst radiating out from the center. In addition, she had peopled the walls with brightly colored mythological beings: friendly sphinxes and griffins in various sizes and various stages of completion, the apartment being, by design, a work in progress. Both magical and festive in the extreme, the whole space exuded an aura of peace, goodwill, and flower power.

It was enough to make Harry vomit.

And Vali, to say the least, gave a hell of a party. The Velvet Underground were performing, and all the beautiful people were dancing. A light show was filtering onto the band through a haze of pot smoke and incense. Warhol and his crew were filming. The air was hot and sweaty

191

with the stench of drug-stoked desire, as couples came together and kissed and groped, fell amorously entwined upon one of the chairs or couches, or skipped off hand in hand for more private assignations. It was a festival of love, a celebration of life, a cross between a Be-In and a Happening, with a pinch of Exploding Plastic Inevitable and a dash of Plato's Retreat thrown in for good measure.

I've cursed this building repeatedly over the years, Harry thought disgustedly, as he entered the apartment, *What the hell gives?* Apparently, he had been mistaken in believing that his malignant influence reigned supreme over the cavernous, dimly lit halls of the Chelsea Hotel.

The party was a star-studded affair: Warhol was surrounded by his entire entourage of Superstars and resident Chelsea Girls, such as Candy Darling and Holly Woodlawn. Allen Ginsberg was there, as was William Burroughs, who lived at the hotel. Corso—who was momentarily out of commission—lived there, as well. Bob Dylan, who usually holed up in Room 211, was busy trying to impress a silver-mini-skirted Edie Sedgwick. Arthur Miller, who lived down the hall, stuck his head in briefly to see what all the commotion was and ended up having a couple of drinks. His friend, the Irish writer, Brendan Behan—run out of every hotel in New York except this one—had already downed more than a couple and was passed out dead-drunk on the couch. Cristo was trying to wrap one of the chairs. And everyone, even the generally crabby Valerie Solanas, seemed to be having an extraordinarily good time.

Utterly nauseating, Harry thought, shaking his head in dismay.

He purposely knocked a drink out of Ginsberg's hand—and Ginsberg apologized to him! It was maddening. Some insidious magical brainwashing spell had obviously been cast, Harry concluded, to make these people so joyful. And although the exact nature of the spell was for the moment hidden from him, he'd be damned if he fell under its influence. He tripped up a couple of the dancers, and they went down in a heap.

Harry threw elbows right and left with malignant intent, as he made his way through the crowd looking for the liquor. "How the hell did this *supposed* witch get such a great apartment, when I'm living in a rundown hellhole?!" Harry asked of no one in particular.

"Maybe she pays for it," Leticia, who was following in his wake, suggested.

"What are you, nuts? Why am I surrounded by imbeciles?" For the time and place—it was, after all, the Chelsea Hotel in the sixties—the idea seemed rather far-fetched. "I'm marching right down to the front desk Monday morning and demanding the best suite in the house!" The author of *Naked Lunch* came up and greeted Harry warmly, and Harry, without any other acknowledgment, grabbed the drink from Burroughs' hand and downed it at a gulp, then dashed the glass to the floor. Glancing right and left, Harry continued, "And speaking of imbeciles, where the hell's Chuck?" As he said this, he caught sight of Chuck over in the very midst of Warhol's entourage, making out with the drag queen, Candy Darling. This incensed Harry. "Traitor! Well, let him work for that two-bit hack! See if I care!"

While it's clear that Harry considered the silver-haired pop artist to be the competition, as the vehemence of his outburst suggests, there was a much deeper reason for Harry's irritation. For although Harry's malaise was best characterized as a terrible and abiding regret that he could never share in the general merriment of his fellows, this feeling was rooted in sexual frustration, as the source of Harry's considerable personal power, of his artistic genius and his charisma—as well as his mastery of the physical and spiritual world through sorcery—lay in his sexual abstinence. Now into his forties, Harry remained a virgin. This was a choice on his part, the result of a conscious decision he had made as an adolescent and had maintained ever since through the exercise of his formidable will. Thus, doomed to remain forever on the sidelines in the drama of life and love, Harry wanted the world to pay for doing this to him—even if he *had* done it to himself! He wanted all mankind to be as miserable as he was, and so he sought to cast a dark, Satanic pall over the lives of his fellows, to overshadow and consume them all in his mighty wrath.

Leticia sensed the reason for Harry's frustration, and she felt that one day he would have enough of this vain pursuit and fall into her waiting arms. In the meantime, a bit of a sorcerer herself, she knew just which buttons to push to make things interesting. "Well, at least the music's good," she said.

Yes, she's right; the music's very good, Harry mused, feeling his muscles relax, as the tension in his face and body dropped away. A connoisseur and an expert, Harry turned his attention to the music, searching in the melody and rhythm for clues he could use to combat Vali's spell. The Velvet Underground were actually kind of depressive, Harry reflected, and that's why he liked them; they were always so aloof and cool. But now, Harry noticed that on this particular night, even Lou and Nico and the rest seemed to have been swept up in the hippie-dippy love-and-peace vibe and were smiling and acting goofy—and starting to sound (*quelle horreur!*) like the Grateful Dead! And this realization frightened Harry. He felt his foot tapping in time to the compromised beat, and thought, *Oh, my God, it's infecting me, too! Worming its way into my brain! And who knows what insidious damage it has already done to my subconscious mind!* The spell was much stronger than Harry had previously suspected. He had to do something quickly to reassert control.

(*Ha!* Leticia thought, when she saw Harry's confused reaction. *With any luck, he'll bust up this party before he even lays eyes on that horrible witch!*)

Harry made his way through the crowd to the wall and located the power cables. He gathered them up and jerked, but they seemed to be caught on something, so he followed them to where they snaked behind a couch and popped back out on the other side, only to disappear beneath the snack table. He spied a bread knife on the table and snatched it up, intending to saw through the cables and put an end to this rock 'n' roll fiasco once and for all. But then, bending to attack the cables, he thought, *Wait a minute, won't I just electrocute myself?* And while that would have likely put an end to the party, Harry was not quite ready to become a martyr to the cause of saving the youth of America from the Demon Rock. Instead, the little sorcerer figured he'd better pull the plugs out of the wall first, and then he could hack through them in relative leisure. He tugged. Damn, still stuck on something! Flipping up the plastic tablecloth, he saw what the obstruction was: two naked hippies were locked in the act of coitus—or, in the parlance of the day, balling—right on top of the cords.

"This floor's taken, dude," the hippie man said.

Thinking to scope out a better angle on the situation, Harry worked his way around to the front of the table and peeked under the tablecloth again. The man's ass was oscillating, piston-like, right in front of the plugs. Harry saw that he could make a grab for them when the man was in his downward thrust, but the slightest miscue would clearly result in a handful of hairy hippie ass. He timed the man's gyrations—lingering overlong on the view in order to further embitter himself with the thought that he could never know such intimacy—then made a stab. Ass.

"Can I help you, man?" the hippie man said.

"Just looking," Harry replied. *I need a drink for this*, he thought, rising up again. Spying a bottle of whiskey on the table, he snatched it up and took a long pull.

But if the liquor helped Harry to forget his troubles (and the couple under the table), it was only momentary. A mean drunk, he immediately started to drink himself into a state of heightened rage. Where was that presumptuous witch? He'd fix her for horning in on his scene—but first he had to get good and plastered. Liquor, he felt, was the source of much of his power, and the more he drank, the madder he became—until he was stomping around in a circle like Rumpelstiltskin. *Who is this witch to trespass on my turf! She must think she's some pretty hot shit to imagine she can take on the great Harry Smith! Aren't those hippies through screwing yet?!*

"Goddamn it!" Harry cursed aloud, "'Heroin' sounds like 'Sugar Magnolia'!"

Leticia came up to throw fuel on the fire. "Oh look, Harry!" she cried out in glee. "Isn't that groovy! They're filming the party! Maybe we'll get to be in a Warhol film!"

Harry noticed the camera set up on the other side of the room, trained on the band. "A film? Is that what's going on around here? That charlatan! I can't believe he tries to call himself a filmmaker. Have you seen his so-called 'films'? A guy sleeping, for God's sake, or six hours of the Empire State Building!"

"We went to that one together, Harry. It was our first date, a double feature. You slept all the way through it, resting your little head on my shoulder. It was so cute."

"I'm the only filmmaker here!" Harry proclaimed bombastically. "I paid a dollar for that ticket, and I'm gonna demand my money back *right now*."

"Actually, I was the one who paid," Leticia pointed out.

Due to previous unpleasant encounters, Warhol's entourage was under strict orders never to let Harry near Andy. In fact, there were pictures of Harry tacked up on the walls of the Factory, with the word BANNED stamped across his face. Consequently, the drag queen, Candy Darling, dressed to the nines in evening gown and heels, interposed herself between Harry and Warhol, who, having caught a glimpse of the unpopular sorcerer making his way through the crowd, cowered behind his camera.

"Let me stop you right there, honey," Candy said. "Andy is busy right now. Can I help you with something?" A striking, statuesque blonde, Candy towered over the diminutive Harry.

"What?! Who the hell are you?!" Harry bellowed, not at all intimidated.

"Why, darling, I'm Candy Darling. But of course."

"Yeah, right! And I'm Soda-Pop Sweetheart. Weren't you the one who was just making out with my cameraman?"

"In your dreams, honey."

"Yeah, well, hands off," Harry said. "Warhol's got enough sycophants in his cult without having to steal mine."

"Oh, my God, little man," Candy said, wrinkling her nose in disgust. "You're stinking."

"What?!"

"Don't you ever bathe?"

"I'll show you!" Harry glanced around, took hold of the curtains, and with a mighty yank, pulled them down, heavy brass rod and all, hitting Candy in the head and knocking her wig askew.

Candy put her hand to her head and brought it away covered in blood. "Christ, I'm bleeding. You repugnant little troll. Where's the make-up girl?"

Harry thought to take this opportunity to slip by her and get to Warhol, but Candy was not finished yet. She grabbed Harry by the collar, straightened him up, and let him have it: a mighty right hook, straight to the teeth.

A minute later, back at the snack table, Leticia dabbed at a dazed Harry's cut lip with some napkins. "There, there, Harry, don't worry. We'll get that nasty old drag queen back. She lives somewhere in this building, and I'm pretty sure she has a cat."

While Harry was busy feeling sorry for himself, the evening's hostess emerged from the bedroom, her flowing gypsy robes in a state of dishevelment, her make-up slightly smeared. Beautiful and vibrant with her wild mane of wavy, red hair, bare-armed and barefoot with bells and bangles dangling from wrists and ankles, Vali gave off a spiritual light that immediately brightened the room. The hippie-Earth-mother-goddess incarnate, with firm yet pendulous breasts and fertile, childbearing hips, she was every young man's dream. Hell, every *old* man's dream. As she flitted and skipped about the place, greeting guests, hugging and kissing and dancing with them, popping into the kitchen now and again to tend a fragrant pot of psychedelic love-stew, it became clear to Harry that it was Vali's sunny influence, her radiant aura, that—more so than any spell—had all along been the source of the mysterious mood of love and good cheer that pervaded the party. Harry was speechless with awe and admiration, and with what he first mistook for hatred. What he found so obnoxious about Vali was her remarkable gaiety, the likes of which, having himself always been morose and depressive, he failed utterly to comprehend. All he knew was that he wanted Vali dead. It was a case of love at first sight.

Vali disturbed Harry's equilibrium, for he felt himself strangely diminished in her presence. Obviously, she had a much better entourage than he, and he suspected that she was considerably further advanced in the dark arts, as well. Though he was unfamiliar with her exact species of witch, he could tell from the vibe—not to mention her appearance—that she was obviously not an ugly, wicked one, as Leticia had maintained. Perhaps she was a succubus of some sort, or a fallen angel. Maybe even a primal Earth spirit, Harry speculated, his imagination running wild. Although his instincts told him to flee, his will restrained him, for he wanted, above all else, to understand this strange being. Throughout his life, Harry's guiding design had been to dominate, to make the world over in his own image, and yet, here was someone whom he could never hope to control.

Harry's feelings were complicated even further when a handsome, young priest with a huge grin on his face emerged from the bedroom only moments after Vali, having obviously enjoyed a satisfying erotic encounter. A Frenchman with coal-dark hair and raffish good looks, Father Fabio had allowed Vali to turn him aside from the path of righteousness, and now gladly followed her down the primrose path to sin and damnation. Recently defrocked as a result of his transgressions, the former good father was unshaven and wore a threadbare old cassock, earning his meager living by selling counterfeit indulgences on the street. But such is the price of love. He was Vali's present favorite—her sex-slave, actually, whom she had enchanted with her beauty. Witnessing the happiness of the love-besotted ex-clergyman, Harry bared his teeth, as he was consumed with an unfamiliar feeling that could only be called jealousy.

When Harry saw the priest embrace and kiss Vali, that was the last straw. He gnashed his teeth in torment. "That witch doesn't deserve such a great apartment!" he declared—somewhat off-topic, but like most New Yorkers, housing issues were always foremost in his mind. "I'm trashing it!" As Leticia skipped nimbly out of the way, he swept the food from the snack table with a mighty swipe of his arm. Seizing the punchbowl and crying out, "Whoops! Sorry!" he sloshed it on the couple under the table. Laughing maniacally, he then overturned the table itself, exposing the dripping-wet couple—who had been contentedly enjoying a post-coital cigarette. Harry grabbed a lamp and threw it out the window, followed by the stereo, then the TV, which exploded into shards of glass and plastic on the sidewalk six floors below. He smashed full glasses of wine and beer and plates of food against the walls. He kicked Corso in the crotch again. Still, everybody was in such a good mood that they scarcely paid Harry any mind.

"Look at that silly, little man!" Warhol-Superstar Edie Sedgwick chirped, giggling girlishly. "He's so angry!"

This enraged Harry all the more. He went into the kitchen and threw the toaster out the window, then the contents of the silverware drawer. He tried to lift the bubbling cauldron of psychedelic love-stew from the stove, but it was much too heavy, so he got a pan and ladled it out, slinging portions of the hot, spicy liquid onto the walls and out the window.

196

The people walking by out on 23rd Street didn't think it was so funny when knives and forks and stew and TVs came crashing down around them, and so it wasn't long before someone called the police. The partygoers heard the sirens coming, growing much louder when the police car turned onto the block, then cutting out abruptly in front of the hotel. A few people filtered out into the hall, ready to make a quick getaway should the situation devolve into head-busting and arrests.

"The cops are coming, Harry!" Leticia called out in warning.

"I hate cops!" Harry said, pausing in his attempt to stuff the snack table out the window. Though he had heard the sirens, their meaning had, until that moment, failed to register.

"And you hate jail even worse!"

"Oh, my God, you're right!" Harry cried out in fright. He gave up on the bent and mangled table, leaving it hanging halfway out the window. Scanning the suddenly less-crowded, less-festive party room for his cameraman/bodyguard, he commanded, "Beat them up, Chuck!"

But Chuck was lounging in a drug-induced stupor on the couch, his arm around Holly Woodlawn, and he showed no inclination to engage in any course of action—suicidal or otherwise.

"Hurry up, Harry! You've got to get away!" Leticia said, tugging on his sleeve.

But it was too late. Two big cops, one Italian and one Irish, strolled into the room. "Hey, what's with all this stuff you guys are throwing out on the street?!" the bigger one, the Italian cop, bellowed. "What's the matter with you! You crazy? What do ya think this is, a nuthouse?"

"Quick!" Leticia said, pulling the terrified Harry along. "In here!" She shoved Harry into Vali's bedroom, switching off the light. "Hide under the bed, and I'll try to keep them out."

Safe behind the locked door, Harry managed to regain a measure of his composure. There was no way he was going to hide under a bed, no way he was going to humiliate himself to that extent just because of a couple of dumb cops. Still, not willing to take any chances, he tried to push Vali's large dresser in front of the door, and, failing in that, propped a chair against the handle, instead. He was going through the vials of magical elixirs, love potions, and anti-aging creams that he had discovered on Vali's dresser, pocketing several, when a small rabbit—none other than Vali's familiar—hopped out of the shadows in the corner and crouched, ears twitching menacingly, in the thin shaft of moonlight.

Letting out a yelp, Harry dove for cover under the bed. There in the darkness, shivering with fear and sneezing from the dust, Harry swore revenge on the rabbit—his mind working feverishly to concoct previously undreamt-of, and of course diabolical, Voodoo experiments—but also, more importantly, revenge on Vali. And he would have it, too, in spades. For Harry was destined within a year's time to make Vali his bride in a ceremony that would shock the world—revolting many, while titillating Satan's elect. The rabbit—whose name, by the way, was Rupert—would prove a more formidable adversary.

The Killing Fields

R. JOSEPH CAPET

Your voice is iron churchbells
cast from Peter's shattered cannon,
pealing volleys
on the ruined land
that blooms again
beneath your tranquil, trampling feet.

Your feet are flowers in the train
of Robert Burns' careless plow,
preaching
to the painted lilies
the lessons of Ecclesiastes
dried from Gaia's cheeks in yours.

Your cheeks are shining cupolas
on churches built by communists
along the Volga—
an atonement
made by laborers whose hands
once folded like the wings of doves.

Your hands are peacocks
living wild
in the gardens
of the Rajputs,
bearing still the thousand bindis
of as many ended generations.

Your eyes are rain
poured out upon the plains
of Jena
to wash away the bloody tide
of history that brought you forth—
the bodies strewn to make your path.

Your body is a library
like Alexander's—
a record
of the countless ages
and all the things that went extinct
before Adam gave them names.

Oh, my love, your name is as a wall
upon the Killing Fields
where God snuffed out the lives
of a thousand
million men
to bring you into mine.

High-Dollar Vaticanus Boys

DAVID S. POINTER

Unknotting economic history's
Lies, omissions, and debris is
Not as easy as excavating a
Kickapoo Indian oil can on
Some ghost-road reservation.
And you can investigate the
World as Ignatius of Antioch
Might have interviewed every
Goat herder or tribal merchant
Around, but to step into the
Pillars between cultivated greed
Where swift intentions, actions,
Consensus, and taboo conspiracy
Coexist black as Victorian-era
Stovepipe polish, you might
Need to insert a Rockefeller
Into your poem, buying up
American medical schools in
The early 1900s before super-
Imposing his skill and monetary
Will upon the co-opted FDA,
All agreeing that a sick society
Is more profitable than a healthy
One, excluding professional
Stenographers while each
Empire protector in attendance
Became his own Athanasius of
Alexandria rewriting history
Like an ancient Biblical scribe.

John Rockefeller

Throw the Bones of Your Mother behind You

L. S. BASSEN

I looked up from my drawing into the blinding sunlight but could not see more than the shapes of the bodies speaking above me. Among the dark, deep voices speaking rapid Greek was a familiar woman's voice also speaking in that strange language, all oo's and k's and plosive p's. I could not understand what the problem was, but any fool could hear there was a problem. Beside me in the trench dug ten feet into this archeological earth was another member of the Brit team, a girl in her twenties, named Juliet. She and I got on only civilly because she was a London-type, and I was a Scot she nicknamed 'Burr,' more I think for my temperament than my thick accent. I was sketching Juliet's dig, the wall, out of which were emerging large decorated jars and something that, at this early stage, looked like a shelf. Juliet could speak Greek.

She translated, "We can't go into the fields because you are raising the dead. In the early morning, we go to pick tomatoes and see the bright light before the sun rises over—solid bodies—carrying shields above their heads. They are all white and go away from the sun toward the west."

"Who are they?" I asked Juliet.

She shushed me, threatening me with the brush. A different voice, official-sounding, spoke above us then. "The police," Juliet said. "Taking this seriously. Agreement with Athens not to disturb the quality of life on Santorini—"

"Tell that to the dogs who own this island—"

"Shh!"

Then again came the voice that could silence me. The American professor who was the director of the expedition, Irene Demas. She had my left upper incisor in her shorts pocket.

"We will, of course, do all we can," Juliet translated, "to stop—to eliminate—this disturbance." A peasant's deep voice interrupted, and Juliet continued, "What? You must stop the digging! My vines will not grow under ghost—under the feet of ghosts!"

Irene's voice replied, drifting down out of the murderous sunlight like a cool breeze. Juliet's back straightened as she translated: "We will watch. Today, we will stop our work. Then, we will try to understand and —" Juliet turned to me, at a loss for words. "It's like 'make amends,' I think, but I don't know the expression. There are lambs in it."

The police official spoke in English, "You will stop the excavation?"

"I will watch, myself, tonight," Irene repeated. "This is your island. We are guests in your home."

The official next spoke in Greek too guttural and rapid for Juliet to translate. But she had no trouble with the farmer's thanks, "*Efkaristo, sas efkaristo poli.*"

I climbed out of the trench, letting Irene see I was there, but keeping a proper distance as the group leaders joined her. There were my Brit boss and a professor from Athens, assistant to the really big shot whose idea Irene had been able to marshal the American money to realize. Because what we were all doing in the 1960s on the Cycladic island of Santorini/Thera, in the best and hottest summer of my life, was digging up Atlantis.

In the *Timaeus*, Plato told the story about a divinely circular island in the western ocean. 'But afterwards there occurred violent earthquakes and floods; and in a single day and night of misfortune ... the island of Atlantis ... disappeared in the depths of the sea.' The big shot from Athens was a seismologist who had reported his findings of a 16th-century B.C.E. volcanic eruption on an island sixty miles north of Crete. The tidal wave from the Atlantis eruption had been anywhere from 200 to 750 feet high when it hit land all around the eastern Mediterranean. The Athenian also theorized that the Atlantis explosion explained the lowering and rising of coastal water described in Exodus. In other words, the eruption at Atlantis (five times stronger than Krakatoa) was the apocalyptic event of the ancient world, remembered in the fundamental stories of Western civilization. When Atlantis exploded, drowning surrounding islands and most of Crete, it became the first place where the end of the world began.

Greece was in the midst of a coup d'état, and the big shot in Athens hadn't been able to get funding to prove his theories. Enter Professor Irene Demas, now with my incisor in her pocket. The States were having their own imperial problems in Southeast Asia at the time, but from what I could understand, the war only made the country richer. As a most-junior assistant professor in scientific illustration at Cambridge, I was blissfully ignorant of all these matters until impressed into service (easily tempted by a fantastic summer salary) to join the Cambridge part of the archeological expedition. There were landfolk from the States and Britain and Athens, and American seafolk with astonishing tech equipment from the Woods Hole Oceanographic Labs, ships and seismologists, scientists, archeologists, mythologists, photographers, and lucky me, the one with the colored pens and pencils and expensive paper all paid for by the Americans.

In the afternoon of the morning of the haunted peasants, when work had been called off, Professor Demas located me deep within one of the cliff caves where I daily went during lunch-siesta, pretending to sketch, though actually sipping bottled water and sleeping on a colorful woolen throw rug bought for that purpose.

Irene said, "I need a bodyguard for tonight."

She was nearly 50 then; I was 27. She was five feet tall and thin as a boy except for the curve of her hips and braless breasts. In the gray pumice cave, blinding noon light outside, relief within, she wore her brown hair braided and coiled like a crown, gray at the temples like her eyes. Irene

Demas was far too small to appear commanding. But I had seen her calm wild dogs with words in their language, which only possibly was Greek. She had seen me with the three Athens toughs who'd tried to mug her on our first night in Greece before the expedition had flown over to Thera.

Then, I only knew her by sight from the plane trip from London. We'd arrived in Athens midday and had spent most of the afternoon getting to our hotel and reaffirming arrangements for the flight to the island. I was glad to let the grownups take care of all of it and to try my luck with Juliet, the result of which was that I slept alone the rest of that afternoon into evening and was nudged awake by my roommate, John, an overeducated fellow from Cornwall eager for companionship for dinner in a strange city. At night it felt as hot as noon, well, in Britain. Nothing is as hot as an Athenian July noon. The crowded, noisy, and altogether hideously modern streets were a great disappointment. Like any first-time tourist to Athens, I imagined I would be traveling back in time, as well as space. John and I ate some oily food and drank some mentholated wine. I quickly had enough of everything and abandoned John to his own devices, assisting him in his subsequent description of me as a stereotypically sociopathic Scot.

I became utterly lost in trying to regain the hotel. Thankfully, some American college kids, cockier even than I, approached me with their instant coffee camaraderie and correctly directed me. I remember alleys of whitewashed stone, stinks of strange foods and organic fluids, and above all, the nauseating sounds of an alien language closing in on me. People leaned out of windows. Everywhere there were second-story balconies like those unearthed on Thera.

Then I saw a tiny woman in a long, khaki skirt and white blouse walking ahead of me. She had a sweater or shawl tied around her shoulders. Self-possessed, holding her sack close to her body. I heard footsteps behind me. The three teens were not after me; the woman was easier. I recognized her as the American professor. The boys ran past me, waving me off with threats I didn't need to translate. They blocked her path. She spoke to them in cool-toned Greek, and maybe she would have handled them as ably as she did the dogs on Thera, but I saw one of them lean in for her sack.

I expected to fight. There were three of them, but they only intended to rob, and I was ready to kill. So, fists and some feet, and a whistle!—that was Irene; she was blowing a piercing whistle, it seemed, right into my ear—I got two of the three down quickly, not interested in getting up again. I was sweating, and it was so hot. I drank the blood in my mouth like water. I faced the third teddy boy whose surprise, like his pals', had turned into fear. I hit him easily; his hands were up in protest, not in fists. *"Parakalo, parakalo,"* he kept crying. The three of them lay on the stone street. People were above, calling out, some curses, some cheers (Irene translated later.), and there was Irene, holding a small shiny revolver in her left hand. American woman! She knelt and picked up a bloody tooth from the ground. My incisor. She wrapped it in a tissue from her sack and placed my tooth in her skirt pocket. Shortly after, at a hospital emergency clinic, she offered it to a dental surgeon. She told me she had retrieved it for this reason, but I already knew better about that woman. She had an eye for bones.

Back in the gray Theran cave, I said, "You don't need a bodyguard against Minoan ghosts or anything else."

"The report of a woman alone would not be believed. The men chose you to accompany me."

"Should I believe you?" For the first time, Irene looked surprised by something I said. "There are fifty underlings you could have sent on this errand," I added.

Irene looked around at the cave, always evaluating. "I'm what they call in the States a micromanager. My husband, of course, called it something else."

She wore no ring. And noticed my glance. "Where, tonight?" I said.

From her shorts pocket, she took a hand-drawn—my work—map of the site and pointed to a group of huge, flat blocks believed to have been part of a palace wall or, possibly, temple altar stones. I nodded in compliance. At the cave entrance, which was a natural opening in the rock cliff that, over centuries, had been bricked into formal arches appropriate to the religious rituals inside the caves, the professor paused, almost as if she could see herself from my perspective, doubly framed by archway and the sunshine outside. Her face was completely hidden in shadow, her form haloed in white light. Again, only her voice reached me.

"I was disappointed in Athens," she said carefully. Her American accent sounded scraped shear, like a sheep. "I was disappointed," she repeated, "to find the violence, your protection, erotic. But it was the men who chose you because you act more like a bodyguard than an academic."

Her unease managed to make it sound like an insult as much as a compliment. Then, the space she had darkly filled was empty and became a brilliant doorway.

That cadmium white light revolves in my memory into the matte black spinel of that Theran night. It felt different from other nights when I had swum in the caldera and lain on a quay, cooled by the *meltami*, the prevailing summer wind that never stopped blowing. But I had been with others and scorned their romantic tales of history and myth. That night, I climbed alone to the Akroteri ruins. I carried a large torch, but it hardly penetrated a darkness that seemed to go back in time as well as space. So I gave up and turned out the light, laying down my sleep rug on one of the wide stones. My searching eyes were relieved by the dotted lights of small houses on the steep hillside below and gloriously above, the stars glittering like reachable diamonds. I had never seen the stars so close. Then, I heard the professor approach before I saw the beam of light from her torch.

I had resolved not to make conversation. Apparently, Irene had made the same decision, so we sat or walked about mutely, separately, for several hours. I watched the zodiac slowly move across the sky. I won. Irene broke the silence. She sounded like an oracle.

"*Kalliste*—most beautiful—was its first name, this island. Jason interpreted the dream of one of his Argonauts on their return with the

Golden Fleece. Jason told Euphemus to throw a handful of earth into the sea. *Kalliste* grew up out of the water from that toss. Euphemus' descendents settled on Lemnos and then Sparta, and finally Theras came here. The island is named *Thera* for him."

"Where did *Santorini* come from?"

"For Saint Irene of Thessalonika. Patron saint of the island." Irene moved into the crossed beams of our torches, which lighted her from below and made deep shadows on her face. "How did you learn to fight like that?" she said.

"Until a month ago, I was illustrating pig dissections and teaching a class frequented as often by anatomy students from the med school as by art students. I learned to fight by being hit. Which is why I left."

Silence. She won. I asked, "You believe the Athenian's theory that Deukalion's flood was the tsunami of the Atlantis eruption?"

"We're trying to excavate the truth."

"I don't understand the archeological quest." In the torchlight, all I could see was her lower torso and the blunted outline of the stones. The sky was close, the ground still gave off heat, and the wind never stopped blowing.

"Neither did my husband. He was more interested in holding on to the future than the past. He married one of his students. Your age, I should guess. The dentist in Athens was amazed by your eyes."

"Did he think I was a *Nea Kameni* vampire?"

Irene laughed.

"That's a yes," I said. "Do you have children?"

"They're teenagers, at camp in their father's custody for the summer. I wondered if your eyes were like a cat's and would reflect light in the dark."

My eyes are a hazel so pale they look yellow, rimmed by remnant RNA for dark brown pigment in three rings. My mutant iris looked, then, like Plato's map of Atlantis before the eruption.

I returned to steadier ground. "There was the Flood. A dove and land. Deukalion went ashore to pray for the restoration of humanity. 'Throw the bones of your mother behind you,' the oracle said. Deukalion—"

"—and his wife, Pyrrha," Irene added.

"—and his wife, Pyrrha, decoded that it meant to throw stones over their shoulders. Where the stones landed, men and women sprang up."

At that moment, at Irene's ankles, I saw two black snakes appear. She felt them and looked down.

"These are harmless," she said, and to my horror, she bent over and took one up in each hand. The crescent moon had risen high enough so that it looked like a crown on her coiled hair, her bare neck as white as the moon. Untrustworthy, re-created memory! The torchlight stayed on the ground, but that is how I remember it, Irene standing like a Minoan goddess, snakes in hand, winding around her bare arms.

We must have slept. I know this: we came awake in the dark with the sense of dawn near. The stars were occluded by cloud. The cow horns of the moon must have passed overhead to the other side of the mountaintop. I was lying on the rug, and Irene was close beside me. I turned. I couldn't see her face. I said, "*Parakalo.* Please."

"*Ne*," she whispered, "yes."

Euripedes wrote: "And in the very surge and breaking of the flood,/ the wave threw up a bull, a fierce and monstrous thing,/ and with his bellowing the land was wholly filled." The bellowing noise was the earthquake. It was the dogs barking that night on Thera. It was my blood pounding in my ears. I saw lightning like no lightning I had seen before, many-branched like a giant tree. It lasted too long, on and on for seconds, for minutes. This lightning was the same that lighted Jason the way through the volcanic cloud's darkness to neighboring Anaphe. The eruption ejected ten cubic miles of island up into the sky so far it was seen and recorded in China. The exhausted island sank 1,300 feet into the sea, forming the beautiful caldera bay where now *varcas* bobbed in the light. Which too came. A brief shower, like a mist, cooled us. Cloud rose off the water, rolling like waves above the waves. It rose up the mountainside over the sleeping white houses tucked into the cliff face, and it floated in the fields that our mountaintop view spread below us. She was small, peaceful on my chest.

"This is where the end of the world began," she said, quiet for more heartbeats, and then she sat up, startled. "Look!"

I followed the line of her snake-bare arm. In a distant field, the cloud-like mists assumed human shapes, and the sky was lighted from beneath the rim of the wine-dark sea. Silver light was turning gold. Then, in a trumpet-like silence, out of the bronzing Mediterranean, the sun rose, huge and whole and round, pink, then as if reddening with arousal.

"It's the mist!" Irene was laughing. "It's the mist!"

The climbing sun rayed down and through the Earth-clouds, making the uppermost layer gleam like blinding metal shields. Irene stood up, her back to me, watching the quickening *meltami* move the mist like a battalion. I found her long skirt on the altar stone. I dug out my lost tooth from her pocket and threw it away behind me.

The mist explanation satisfied the locals. It was the professor's deference to them that mollified the peasants; I doubt anyone in authority had ever treated them with respect before, back to the time before the Minoans had escaped the Flood. Where had they all gone, the 30,000 or more *Kallisteans* whose skeletons were never found but one? One human skeleton and one piglet left alone on all Thera before the end of the world. Who warned them? How did they know? Where did they go? The researchers debated these questions endlessly throughout August as the frantic excavating continued against a deadline and daily threat of the mercurial moods of Greek generals and xenophobes.

I knew. The high priestess had saved her people, directing them to sail to their ports in Phoenicia and Spain, to outposts as far north as England. And millennia later, when the Romans finally came, we fled again farther north and west. Those snakes St. Patrick banished from Éire? Those standing stones in the Orkneys where I summered as a boy? Not the first end of the world at all, the beautiful island thrown into the ancient sea had generated immortal waves.

Ode to the Couches
of the 1950s

A Connecticut housewife confined
By an hourglass idyll once graced this couch,
With charm-school poise, curtsied stems,
Sheaved in hose, crochet hook in hand,

Crowned with Crockett cap or sunbonnet,
Anchored by her apron and womb,
Ankle-cuffed in matrimony to a dubious debt collector
Who fashioned a wine-red smoking jacket

When he nipped an after-dinner liqueur,
Thumbed a packet of racing forms,
His miserly heart choked to an occasional stop
By the stifling grip of a money-clip.

She, starved for affection, continually on the verge
Of quiet tears wept into a cheese cloth,
Prodded into a tacit disorder by days and decades
Of feather-dusting the golden egg, aimlessly pacing,

Waiting in a town with no train station,
For a pot of coffee to percolate, for death, or God
To descend patronly from the attic steps,
Like an eyelash dripping rain. A spot of her

Once-radiant nail polish fell from the speculum,
At the thought of a seamless escape, but we know
The endurable belles and convex dandies
Of the past rest fixed in a state of raw putrefaction.

When we sit we can sense the dead who hibernate
In the couch's embroidered snowflakes,
The bedbugs stupefied and dancing in their castle,
But maybe we will meet this woman

At the climax of a future reincarnation,
Fall in love on an icy lake made of strangers'
Mirrored skates and faces, a fractured city
Frostbitten underneath, not knowing

We had lived there once,
Not knowing we will live there
Again, but finally,
The furniture will be new.

BRIAN LE LAY

Author

[COVER ARTIST:]

Terry Fan

[Ontario, Toronto, Canada] is an illustrator who studied at Ontario College of Art & Design University and went through their interdisciplinary program. He works with ink, graphite, and Adobe Photoshop and is currently involved in a number of creative pursuits, including T-shirt design, screenwriting, graphic novels, and children's book illustration. His motto is short but poignant: "Art is my drug of choice." [society6.com/igo2cairo] [Front cover artwork: "Mr. Sunshine"] [Back cover artwork: "Business as Usual"]

A. Jay Adler

[Los Angeles, California] is one of this issue's Featured Writers. You can find his full biography on page 68. [sadredearth.com] [Featured Writer, pages 68-100]

Diana Andrasi

[Montreal, Quebec, Canada] completed her studies in philology at the University of Bucharest, followed by a master's degree and a PhD in Comparative Literature at the University of Montreal. While research- ing for her doctoral thesis on the subject of thought-image as a poetry device (at the beginning of the 20th century), she became interested in research projects linking contemporary poetry to urban legends, political ideologies, and global cultural development. She's written articles, poems, and essays in both English and French. She lives in the far west of the Montreal Island with all her books and significant ones. [is.gd/DianaAndrasi] [pages 14, 38, 42]

Leah Angstman

[Palo Alto, California] is a transplanted Midwesterner, unsure of what feels like home anymore. She writes historical fiction, poetry, and plays; has had 20 chapbooks published; and has earned two Pushcart Prize nominations. Recently, she won the Loudoun Library Foundation Poetry Contest and Nantucket Directory Poetry Contest and was a placed finalist in the Bevel Summers Prize for Short Fiction (Washington and Lee University), Baltimore Science Fiction Society Poetry Contest, and West Coast Eisteddfod Poetry Competition. Her work has appeared in numerous journals, including *Los Angeles Review of Books*, *The Journal of Compressed Creative Arts*, *Tupelo Quarterly*, *New Mexico Review*, *Midwestern Gothic*, and *Shenandoah*. [leahangstman.com] [pages 6, 114, 142]

L. S. Bassen

[Lincoln, Rhode Island] is a 2011 Finalist for the Flannery O'Connor Short Fiction Award; 2009 winner of the Atlantic Pacific Press Drama Prize; Fiction Editor at *Prick of the Spindle*; poetry and fiction reviewer for Horse Less Press, Small Beer Press, *The Rumpus*, Drexel University's Press 1, *The Brooklyner*, Big Wonderful Press, *Melusine*,

NewPages, and *Galatea Resurrects*; Literary Life blogger at *Sobriquet Magazine*; reader for *Electric Literature*; has had both poetry and fiction published in many literature journals, including *Kenyon Review, American Scholar, Minnetonka*, and *Persimmontree*; and is a prize-winning, produced, and published playwright (Samuel French, ATA in NYC, OH, NC), and commissioned co-author of a WWII memoir by the Scottish bride of Baron Kawasaki. [lsbassen.com] [page 201]

Sean Brendan-Brown

[Olympia, Washington] is a graduate of the Iowa Writers' Workshop. A medically retired Marine, he is the author of three poetry chapbooks (*No Stopping Anytime; King of Wounds; West Is a Golden Paradise*), a fiction chapbook, *Monarch of Hatred*, and a short-story collection, *Brother Dionysus* (MilSpeak Books). He has been published in *Notre Dame Review, Wisconsin Review, Indiana Review, Texas Review, Southampton Review, Poiesis Review*, and in the University of Iowa Press anthologies: *American Diaspora* and *Like Thunder*. He is the recipient of a 1997 NEA Poetry Fellowship and a 2010 NEA Fiction Fellowship. [is.gd/facebookSBB] [page 131]

R. Joseph Capet

[Monmouth, Oregon] is a poet and theologian whose work in multiple languages has appeared in journals and magazines as diverse as *decomP, The Montreal Review, American Journal of Biblical Theology*, and *Sennaciulo*. He currently lays up treasures on earth teaching English to students in Latin America and treasures in heaven teaching Esperanto to anyone who will learn, while serving as poetry editor for *P. Q. Leer*. [pages 54, 123, 198]

Alan Catlin

[Schenectady, New York] has been writing and publishing since the 70s. Among his many publications are some sixty chapbooks and full-length books of poetry and prose. His most recent full-length book of poetry is, *Alien Nation*. He is the poetry editor of *Misfit Magazine*. [misfitmagazine.net] [pages 31, 33, 40]

Christina Elaine Collins

[Fairfax, Virginia] holds an MFA in fiction from George Mason University. Her stories and poems have appeared in various literary periodicals and anthologies, including *Jabberwock Review, Weave Magazine*, and *NonBinary Review*. In addition to three Pushcart Prize nominations, she has received Finalist and Special Mention awards in several literary competitions such as the 2014 Katherine Paterson Prize at *Hunger Mountain*, the *Heavy Feather Review* 2013 Featured Fiction Chapbook Contest, and the *Gambling the Aisle* 2013 Chapbook Competition. She has been a writer-in-residence at the Kimmel Harding Nelson Center for the Arts, as well as the Art Commune program in Armenia. [page 12]

Jesseca Cornelson

[Montgomery, Alabama] is one of this issue's Featured Writers. You can find her full biography on page 170.
[difficulthistory.wordpress.com] [Featured Writer, pages 170-185]

Gary Every

[Cottonwood, Arizona] is the author of nine books, including *Shadow of the Ohshad*, a compilation of the best of his award-winning newspaper columns concerning Southwestern history, folklore, Native Americans, and the environment. His science fiction novella, *The Saint and the Robot*, regarding medieval legend he uncovered about Thomas Aquinas, is also available from Amazon. [garyevery.com] [pages 106, 108, 126]

Ed Hamilton

[New York City, New York] is the author of *Legends of the Chelsea Hotel: Living with the Artists and Outlaws of New York's Rebel Mecca* (Da Capo, 2007) and the short story collection, *The Chintz Age: Tales of Love and Loss for a New New York* (Červená Barva Press, Fall 2015). His fiction has appeared in various journals, including *Limestone Journal, The Journal of Kentucky Studies, River Walk Journal, Exquisite Corpse, Modern Drunkard, Lumpen, Omphalos, Bohemia, Poetic Story: An Anthology,* and in translation in Czechoslovakia's *Host*. His non-fiction has appeared in *Experienced: Rock Music Tales of Fact and Fiction* (Vagabondage Press LLC, 2011), as well as in *Chelsea Now, The Villager, The Huffington Post,* and other local NYC newspapers. [edhamilton.nyc] [page 187]

Anthony G. Herles

[Poughkeepsie, New York] is a retired New York State English teacher. He taught English at the high school level for 30 years and also taught English as an adjunct lecturer for 20 years at Dutchess Community College in Poughkeepsie. His work has appeared in *The New York Times, Happy, PEN Works, Words of Wisdom, New Authors Journal, The Hartford Courant, The Poetry Explosion Newsletter* (PEN), *Barbaric Yawp, New England Writers Network* (NEWN), *The Blind Man's Rainbow, Poiesis Review, Timber Creek Review, River Poets Journal, The Storyteller, Jaw Magazine, The Writer's Post Journal, The Lyric,* and others. Four chapbooks are available from Alternating Current: *Fourteen Singles, Poughkeepsie Icehouse, Men Stuff,* and *Bob Barker Died.* [page 34]

Angie Jeffreys Schomp

[Greensboro, North Carolina] has been writing poetry since the age of six. She studied English Literature and Creative Writing at Hollins University. She also studied linguistics at University College Cork, Cork, Ireland, for one lucky semester. Angie now cares for her father's health full time. Since college, she has worked for Open Hand Publishing, LLC, tended the flocks at a public school after-school care program, privately nannied for a couple years, and chosen to spend most of her spare time gardening and hanging with her dog. Strangely, this timeline lends itself to lots of the good, bad, sometimes the ugly, too, in writing. Enjoy. [suburbanscrawlr.com] [page 43-53]

Luther Jett

[Washington Grove, Maryland] has recently completed his first novel. His poetry has been published in numerous journals, including *The GW Review, ABRAXAS, Beltway, Innisfree,* and *Main Street Rag*. His poetry performance piece, "Flying to America," debuted at the 2009 Capital Fringe Festival in Washington D.C. He was also a winner in the 2011 Moving Words Poetry Competition in Arlington, Virginia. [lutherjett.com] [pages 17, 36, 130, 169]

Miodrag Kojadinović

[Belgrade, Serbia] is a Canadian-Serbian poet, prose writer, journalist, translator, interpreter, and photographer. He has undergraduate degrees from Serbia and Canada, postgraduate ones from Serbia, the U.S., the Netherlands, and Hungary, and has worked at universities/colleges in Norway, Mainland China, the Netherlands, Serbia, and Macau. His writing, in a wide range of genres, has been published in thirteen languages in Canada, Serbia, the U.S., France, Russia, China, England, Holland, Spain, Slovenia, India, Macau, Scotland, Croatia, Australia, Germany, Israel, Austria, and Montenegro. He has also appeared in three documentaries (one of which was about himself as a globetrotter seeking a place under the Sun). [wikipedia.org/wiki/Miodrag_Kojadinović] [pages 24-30]

Phillip Larrea

[Sacramento, California] has been widely published in the U.S., Canada, Ireland, and Europe. His chapbook, *Our Patch* (Writing Knights Press), was released January 2013. Phillip's full-length poetry collection, *We the People* (Cold River Press), was released in April 2013. [is.gd/WeThePeople] [pages 145, 146, 147]

Brian Le Lay

[Boston, Massachusetts] is a poet and a sociology student. His poems have recently appeared in *The Orange Room Review*, *Word Riot*, and *Gutter Eloquence*. [conceiveyourself.blogspot.com] [pages 148, 207]

Lyn Lifshin

[Vienna, Virginia] has written more than 125 books and edited four anthologies of women writers. Her poems have appeared in numerous poetry and literary magazines in the U.S., and she has given more than 700 readings. Lyn has appeared at Dartmouth, Skidmore, Cornell University, Shakespeare Library, Whitney Museum, and Huntington Library and has been Poet-in-Residence at the University of Rochester,

Antioch, and Colorado Mountain College. She is the winner of numerous awards, including the Jack Kerouac Award for her book, *Kiss the Skin Off*. She is also the author of *Another Woman Who Looks Like Me* (Black Sparrow Press), the prize-winning *The Licorice Daughter: My Year with Ruffian* (Texas Review Press), *Before It's Light* (Black Sparrow), *Cold Comfort* (Black Sparrow), *Persephone* (Red Hen), *A Girl Goes into the Woods* (NYQ Books), and many more. [lynlifshin.com] [pages 11, 101, 168]

Helen Losse

[Winston-Salem, North Carolina] is the author of three full-length poetry books, *Facing a Lonely West* and *Seriously Dangerous* (Main Street Rag), and *Better with Friends* (Rank Stranger Press), and three chapbooks. A former English teacher, Helen has been nominated twice for a Pushcart Prize and three times for a Best of the Net award, one time of which she was a finalist. She was Poetry Editor for *The Dead Mule School of Southern Literature* and is now its Poetry Editor Emeritus. Her poems have been anthologized in *In the Arms of Words: Poems for Disaster Relief*, *Washing the Color of Water Golden: A Hurricane Katrina Anthology*; and *Literary Trails of the North Carolina Piedmont*. She holds a BSE from Missouri Southern State University and an MALS from Wake Forest, where she wrote her thesis on Martin Luther King, Jr. [helenl.wordpress.com] [page 127]

Heather K. Michon

[Palmyra, Virginia] is an essayist and historian living in the green hills of Central Virginia. Her work has appeared in Salon.com, *The Washington Post*, and other publications. Her essay, "The Night Watch: Creativity in the Dim," developed out of new research on the effect of dim light on creativity, but turned into a short historical survey on just how much human artistry has been born and nurtured, mushroom-like, in the dark. [about.me/heathermichon] [page 138]

James O'Brien

[New York City, New York] holds a PhD in Editorial Studies from the Editorial Institute at Boston University, where he researched and edited Bob Dylan's other-than-song writings. He is engaged in a bibliography for Oxford University Press, covering writings about the filmmaker John Cassavetes. His journalism, short stories, and poetry are published in numerous journals and magazines. [jamesobrien.cc] [page 56]

Robert L. Penick

[Louisville, Kentucky] has had poetry, prose, and essays appear in over 100 literary magazines, including *The Hudson Review, The North American Review,* and *Quiddity.* He works with the mentally ill in Louisville. [f:/robert.l.penick.9] [page 124]

Pearl Pirie

[Ottawa, Ontario, Canada] is a food columnist, a book reviewer, and the author of three full-length collections of poetry: *the pet radish, shrunken* (BookThug, 2015), *been shed bore* (2010), and *Thirsts* (2011), the latter of which won the Robert Kroetsch Award for Innovative Poetry. She has a micropress called *phafours.* [pearlpirie.com] [page 128]

David S. Pointer

[Murfreesboro, Tennessee] is an American political poet. In Spring 2012, he was asked to become an advisory panel member at Writing For Peace. This organization teaches world peace writing to young people ages 13-19. David's two most recent political poetry books are *The Psychobilly Princess* and *Sundrenched Nanosilver.* His recent anthology publications include: *Serial Killers 2, Poe-It!, Poiesis Review,* and elsewhere. [f:/david.s.pointer] [pages 105, 111, 186, 200]

Claudia Serea

[Rutherford, New Jersey] is a Romanian-born poet who immigrated to the U.S. in 1995. Her poems and translations have appeared in *5 a.m., Meridian, Harpur Palate, Word Riot, The Red Wheelbarrow, Apple Valley Review,* and many others. She was nominated two times for the Pushcart Prize and Best of the Net. She is the author of *Angels & Beasts* (Phoenicia Publishing, Canada, 2012), *A Dirt Road Hangs from the Sky* (8th House Publishing, Canada), and the chapbooks: *The System* (Cold Hub Press, New Zealand, 2012), *With the Strike of a Match* (White Knuckles Press, 2011), and *Eternity's Orthography* (Finishing Line Press, 2007). She co-edited and co-translated *The Vanishing Point That Whistles: An Anthology of Contemporary Romanian Poetry* (Talisman Publishing, 2011), and translated from the Romanian, Adina Dabija's *Beautybeast* (Northshore Press, 2012). [cserea.tumblr.com] [page 18]

Kirby Anne Snell

[Chapel Hill, North Carolina] has had poems published in *Crab Orchard Review, Flyway, Measure,* and *Think Journal.* She received her MFA in Poetry from the University of North Carolina–Wilmington. A Returned Peace Corps Volunteer (Micronesia, 2009-2011), Kirby currently works as an editor. [t:/KirbyAnneWrites] [page 117]

Alex Stolis

[Minneapolis, Minnesota] has had poems published in numerous journals. He is the author of *Justice for All* (Conversation Paperpress), a chapbook based on the last words of Texas Death Row inmates, and *A Cabal of Angels* (Red Bird Chapbooks), a collaborative chapbook with artist Susan Solomon. An e-chapbook, *From an iPod found in Canal Park; Duluth, MN,* was also recently released by Right Hand Pointing. He has been the recipient of five Pushcart Nominations. [page 150]

Donovan White

[Lowell, Massachusetts] made a living as a carpenter while enrolled in a Creative Writing program and wrote short fiction on nights and weekends. Then, he worked as an editor and wrote nothing but

headlines and captions. Now, he manages software development and writes poetry on nights and weekends and on breaks in his workday commute. Whenever he starts feeling mature, or smart, or sophisticated, sooner or later he remembers that he's had only a few great loves in his life, and three of them were dogs. His work has surfaced in *Silenced Press*, *Nibble*, *Word Riot*, *Poiesis Review*, and *Durable Goods*, among others.
[f:/donovan.white.165] [page 149]

Laura Elizabeth Woollett

[Melbourne, Victoria, Australia] is a Perth-born author, editor, and aspiring screenwriter. Her first novel, *The Wood of Suicides*, was published in early 2014 by The Permanent Press, and her short story collection, *The Love of a Bad Man*, is currently being considered for publication. Since 2012, she has been a fiction editor for *Voiceworks*.
[lauraelizabethwoollett.com] [page 151]

Elizabeth Zuckerman

[Trenton, New Jersey] has had work published in *Timeless Tales Magazine*, the Pink Narcissus Press anthology, *Rapunzel's Daughters*, and *NonBinary Review*. Her history-teacher parents were thrilled when she learned to enjoy battlefields and historical markers. She lives in Trenton, where she blogs about myths in her free time.
[t:/LizCanTweet] [page 118]

Public Domain Authors

Thomas Carlyle [page 67]; Samuel T. Coleridge [page 64]; Stephen Crane [page 32]; Nicolas de La Caille [page 43]; Ralph Waldo Emerson [page 144]; Robert Frost [page 35]; A. E. Housman [page 37]; Vojislav Ilić [pages 27, 28, 30]; Vachel Lindsay [page 125]; J. H. McKenzie [page 132]; Herman Melville [pages 41, 113]; Edna St. Vincent Millay [page 137]; Sappho [page 37]; William Shakespeare [page 39]; Catherine Warfield [page 112]; William Wordsworth [pages 62, 63]

The Charter Oak

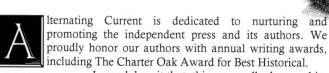

A lternating Current is dedicated to nurturing and promoting the independent press and its authors. We proudly honor our authors with annual writing awards, including The Charter Oak Award for Best Historical.

Legend has it that this unusually large white oak tree on what early colonists named Wyllys Hyll in Hartford, Connecticut, was where the Royal Charter of 1662 was shoved into a hidden hollow to thwart its confiscation by the English governor-general who wished to revoke the piece of legislation that granted autonomy to the colonists. This tree, named the Charter Oak, has since become a symbol of the power of documents and recorded history, the freedom they give us, showcasing the lengths one would go to protect, to defend, and to stand by words that could forever change the course of people's lives. While the Charter Oak is a strong, undeniable piece of American history, its symbol is universal. Words empower us all, the whole world over, and we'll die to protect our collective right to them. Here, at Alternating Current, we want to preserve and reward those words that empower us, so that they, too, may go down in history.

The Charter Oak Award for Best Historical is awarded annually to a single piece of work that is historical in nature and that has been submitted to and published by Alternating Current. All works submitted to Alternating Current are considered for the award and for publication, and we welcome readers to let us know where we can find outstanding historical work of merit so that we may invite those authors to submit their work to us, as well.

The winning piece receives print publication in *Footnote*; online publication on our website; complimentary copies of the *Footnote* print journal with the winning piece indicated with our medallion imprint; a certificate; a cash honorarium; and our virtual medallion with permission for use on the author's websites and/or any published books or online outlets. A second and a third place and nine notable-mention winners receive print publication in *Footnote*; publication on our website and blog; and other prizes. Full submission and award details can be found at alternatingcurrentarts.com.

Alternating Current is pleased to present a select panel of editors, publishers, writing instructors, literary organization members, and/or published authors who are invited by our press to participate in the blind judging process to select the winning pieces each year. The winners are selected by December and announced in January, with the annual release of each issue of *Footnote*. The judging process consists of all submissions being sent blind to the external judging panel, where the finalists and top pieces are determined by those judges via a ranking system. The judges' decisions are final; Alternating Current does not determine the final outcome. Because the winners are judged blind by a panel unaffiliated with Alternating Current, and all of the submissions to our press are also read blind, the press' staff members are eligible to compete for the award, but submission editors are not.

AWARD 2015

2015 Judges

Lynn Alexander

holds degrees in social welfare, nonprofit and arts management, and public policy; is editor and publisher at Full of Crow Press; is author of *Flesh Made Widow* and *Prologue to Mariamne*; is an annual literary-event curator for the Oakland Beast Lit Crawl and the Cleveland Lit Crawl; is co-founder and host of San Francisco's annual Toxic Abatement Poetry Festival; and has published a variety of print zines, hosted radio shows, and edited fiction and poetry for various independent presses.

Harry Calhoun

holds a History Degree from Penn State, where he also minored in Political Science; is the former editor of *Pig in a Poke*, where he published such noted authors as Charles Bukowski, Jim Daniels, and Louis McKee; and is the author of eleven books, including *Failure Is Unimportant*, *Retro*, and *Near daybreak, with a nod to Frost*. He has been published in innumerable publications since 1981, including freelance article writing for hundreds of journals, ranging from *Writer's Digest* to *Mississippi Arts and Letters* to *The National Enquirer*. He is currently a marketing writer for companies such as GE and IBM and is a member of the North Carolina Writers Network.

Paula Cary

is a poet and writer, with pieces published in such journals as *Poiesis Review*, *Nerve Cowboy*, and *Thirteen Myna Birds*; editor of the literary blog *Poet Hound*; and author of *Agapornis Swinderniana* (Dancing Girl Press) and *Sister, Blood and Bone* (Blood Pudding Press).

Jeff Pfaller

is a novelist and short-story writer; co-founder and fiction editor of the literary journal *Midwestern Gothic*; and co-publisher of MG Press—publications that spotlight the gorgeous, but oft-overlooked, Midwest.

Russell Streur

is the operator of *Plum Tree Tavern* and the world's original online poetry bar, *The Camel Saloon*; two-time recipient of awards for excellence from the Georgia Poetry Society; widely published in numerous journals; and author of *The Muse of Many Names* and *Table of Discontents*.

Acknowledgments

 Special acknowledgment and thanks to Devin Byrnes and SuA Kang of Hardly Square, for their creativity in designing our Charter Oak Award medallion imprint. Hardly Square is a strategy-,  branding-, and design-based boutique located in Baltimore, Maryland, that specializes in graphic design, web design, and eLearning courses. Their invaluable design expertise has made our annual awards come to life. Find out more about them at hardlysquare.com.

Alternating Current wishes to acknowledge the following publications where pieces from issue No. 1 first appeared: "The Ballad of Augustin Lafavre" first appeared in *The Eclectic Muse*. "The American Road" first appeared as "The American Road: Route 66 at 80" in *Double Take*. "Bordello Rooms" first appeared in *The Writer's Eye*. "Dingus" first appeared in the *Indiana Crime Anthology*. "Big Daddy Joe" first appeared on *Four-Sep Publications*. "At noon" first appeared in *Durable Goods #79*. "Letter from Thomas Jefferson to John "The Tory" Randolph—1775: A Revolutionary Poem" first appeared in *Our Patch*, *Counterpunch*, *Miracle E-zine*, and *We the People*. "Wrong, Right, and Reasonable" first appeared in *Medusa's Kitchen* and *We the People*.

Bibliography for *Gorsas' Guillotine: A Nonfiction Narrative of Wordsworth and Carlyle*: **1.)** Carlyle, Thomas. *Reminiscences*. C. E. Norton, ed. London and New York: J. M. Dent and E. P. Dutton, 1932. Reprinting the edition of 1887. **2.)** — ——. *The French Revolution: A History*. K. J. Fielding and David Sorensen, eds. Oxford and New York: Oxford University Press, 1989. Reprinting the edition of 1837. **3.)** Froude, James Anthony. *Thomas Carlyle: A History of His Life in London, 1834-1881*. Vol. 1. (St. Clair Shores, Mi.: Scholarly Press, 1970). Reprinting the edition of 1897. **4.)** Gill, Stephen. "Wordsworth, William (1770–1850)." In *Oxford Dictionary of National Biography*, H. C. G. Matthew and Brian Harrison, eds. Oxford: Oxford University Press, 2004. Online ed., edited by Lawrence Goldman, January 2008. http://oxforddnb.com/view/article/29973 (accessed October 20, 2009). **5.)** Gough, Hugh. *The Newspaper Press in the French Revolution*. Chicago: Dorsey Press, 1988. **6.)** Johnston, Kenneth. *The Hidden Wordsworth*. New York: W. W. Norton, 1998. **7.)** Roe, Nicholas. *Wordsworth and Coleridge: The Radical Years*. Oxford: Clarendon Press, 1988. **8.)** Sisman, Adam. *The Friendship: Wordsworth and Coleridge*. New York: Penguin Viking, 2007. **9.)** Stephen, Leslie. "Spedding, James (1808–1881)." Rev. W. A. Sessions. In *Oxford Dictionary of National Biography*, H. C. G. Matthew and Brian Harrison, eds. Oxford: Oxford University Press, 2004. Online ed., edited by Lawrence Goldman, May 2006. http://oxforddnb.com/view/article/26090 (accessed October 20, 2009). **10.)** Wordsworth, Dorothy. *The Grasmere Journals*. Pamela Woof, ed. Oxford: Clarendon Press, 1991. **11.)** Wordsworth, William. *The Prelude: 1799, 1805, 1850*. Jonathan Wordsworth, M. H. Abrams, and Stephen Gill, eds. New York and London: W. W. Norton & Company, 1979.

Colophon

The edition you are holding is the First Edition pressing of this publication.

Our *Footnote* logo is set in an Alternating Current-created font. The number "1," non-standard text of the title pages, interior title fonts, biography name headers, and Charter Oak Award judges headers, are set in Old Newspaper Types by Manfred Klein. The drop capitals are set in Imperator Plaque, created by Paul Lloyd. All other fonts are set in Calisto MT. All fonts are used with permission; all rights reserved.

The number tag on the title pages, the bird cornerpieces, the Charter Oak ribbon for the second and third place medallions, and the scissors separator are in the public domain, courtesy of The Graphics Fairy. The name ribbons and the Charter Oak silhouette are in the public domain, courtesy of Clker. All other photographs and graphics are in the public domain. The Alternating Current lightbulb logo was created by Leah Angstman, ©2015 Alternating Current. The Charter Oak Award medallion imprints were created by SuA Kang and Devin Byrnes of Hardly Square, for Alternating Current's sole use. The QR codes were created with the QR Droid generator (To read QR codes on your smartphone, we recommend downloading QR Droid for Android or Zapper Scanner for iPhone.). The Hardly Square logo is ©Hardly Square, hardlysquare.com. All graphics are used with permission; all rights reserved.

The editors wish to thank the font and graphic creators for allowing legal use.

alternatingcurrentarts.com

29493336R00140

Made in the USA
Middletown, DE
21 February 2016